PARKLAND SPEAKS

SURVIVORS FROM
MARJORY STONEMAN DOUGLAS
SHARE THEIR STORIES

PARKLAND
SPEAKS

Edited by MSD teacher
Sarah Lerner

Crown · New York

To the students, teachers, faculty, and staff of Marjory Stoneman Douglas High School, as well as the families of the seventeen victims and the Parkland and Coral Springs communities, we honor the strength you've shown during these trying times. We have witnessed a tragedy no one should ever have to face, and have come out of it with strength and purpose. We will continue to speak out and fight to make sure nothing like this ever happens again. I hope that this book sheds light on what we went through, and what we will continue to go through for the rest of our lives. We are positive, passionate, proud. We are #MSDStrong.

To my husband, Glen, thanks for supporting me always, and being my biggest fan. I love you and can't imagine doing any of this without you. To my children, David and Hannah, I hope that I've made you proud. I know this journey hasn't been easy, but it's been the most important thing I've ever done. It's all for you. To my parents, Ellen and Mark, thanks for raising me to be strong, outspoken, and fearless. —S.L.

Photo by Kyra Parrow

ReWrite
by Sarah Lerner,
English and journalism teacher at MSD

I've always been a writer.

I love the feel of the keys under my fingers,
clicking as the words appear on the screen.
I love the whole process—creation, editing, revising.
 Lather, rinse, repeat.

For some, writing serves as a way to share who they really are.
A way to be creative, open, fearless, honest.
A way to say what they want, without having to vocalize it.

After tragedy strikes, people respond differently.
Some take pictures. Some find food. Some exercise.
 Some retreat. Some write.

Watching my students find their voices after someone
 tried to silence them was impressive.
Perhaps that's an understatement.
It was awe-inspiring. It was brave. It was courageous.

They turned their grief into words, into pictures, into
 something that helped them begin the healing
 process.
They created something that will be kept for the rest of
 their lives.
A yearbook.

This yearbook is so much more than *just* a book.
It's memories.
It's stories.
It's pictures.
It's smiles.
It's heartache.
It's real.

The theme for the yearbook was "As One," which we
    selected in April 2017.
I couldn't think of anything more fitting for what the year
    became.
We struggled as one.
We loved as one.
We cried as one.
We mourned as one.

I will always be a writer.
I will always love to read other people's writing.
I will always be inspired by the process through which
    people write.

In working on *Parkland Speaks,* I was able to further my
    passion for writing, through the editing process.
I read pieces from my students, as well as students who
    aren't mine.
It is raw.
It is real.
It happened to them.

I am thankful for the opportunity to participate in this
    project.
I am thankful to be able to use my voice.
I am thankful that I work with students who aren't afraid
    to use theirs.

Photo by Kyra Parrow

the words

by anna bayuk

i've been having trouble finding the words.
when you're huddled in a corner with twenty other students,
waiting for if — no, when — a man with a gun will shoot
   through the window,
will reach in to pull open the door handle,
will not spare any of you,
when you are waiting to die,
you lose your own adjectives.
you are no longer yourself,
you are a series of actions.
you are waiting,
you are texting your loved ones that you love them,
you are shaking,
you are holding the hand of a girl you only half knew
like it is a lifeboat,
like it can save you even though you know now that
only chance, only luck, only maybe providence can save you.
you are forgetting to pray.
you never really learned how.
you are staying quiet, no, quieter, no, silent
you are staying silent.
for a moment, i was not silent.
there was a plastic walmart bag full of valentines from
   and for the people that i care about on my lap,
and when i shifted it off to the side so that i could move
   my legs even an inch
it was the loudest thing that i had ever heard and
i had to suppress my cringe on the off chance that it could
   make more sound.

i heard gunshots in the distance.
i heard footsteps in the hallway.
i know now that it was the police, the swat team,
but at the time i thought it was the end.
we were one of the last groups evacuated,

and time passed strangely in those two hours where we
just waited.
i shook.
and i listened.
and i waited.
and i kept silent.
but now, i refuse to stay that way.
this could have been prevented.
this can never happen again.
the numbness has started to crack
and i want my adjectives back
and i want change
and i want change
and i want this to be the last time students became survivors,
where, worse, they became victims.
i knew one of the victims.
her name was jaime.
we had been in the same indian princess group when
we were children.
my father had taught her earth science,
i had peer counseled for the class.
when i heard her name i was just my actions again.
i was crying,
sobbing,
gasping for air.

seventeen people.
coach feis told me to have a nice afternoon as i walked
home from school every day and i know that he meant
it.
it's not fair.
i've been having trouble finding the words.

Inside a Fearful Mind
by Chantal Chalita

A tinge of fear
nestles itself comfortably
between the intricate wiring of my brain.
An idea so absurd,
a laugh manages to escape me.
A shiver running down my spine,
my legs trembling beneath me
and I can't keep up.
Amid the confusion,
the tumultuous chaos
of the screams,
the "Run!"
hearts pounding in synchrony,
and I find myself locked up
within the walls of a classroom closet.
The silence and the piercing apprehension
fill my ears with one of my worst fears—
Doubt.
An uncertainty of reality.
Completely isolated from the entire world,
all I can do is wait.
But a powerful instrument
lies in my hands,

and in the hands of those around me.
A form of communication
bursts with bright flashes and vibrations
at the click of a button.
Thumbs vigorously swarm the screens,
which one by one
illuminate faces with frowns
of the news.
The news that rids us of our doubt
only to fill our void with despair.
We try to check on each other,
making desperate attempts to get an
"I am OK."
And the news keeps coming in.
It doesn't pause
or give you a break.
It keeps hitting you
with debilitating blows,
one after the other,
as those missing responses remain empty,
and your messages remain unread.
Tears begin to stroke my eyes
when I realize one of my messages will remain unread
    forever.

Third Floor
BY JOSEPH DeARCE

On February 14, I was on the third floor of the 1200 building in Mrs. Lippel's creative writing class. It was an average day. The class was lively and spoke of after-school Valentine's Day plans. As usual I was watching YouTube videos on my phone, since I had already completed the Valentine's Day poem assignment. All I could think about was going home and playing video games with my friends.

As the clock hit 2:30, everyone began to pack up. I was still watching the video when suddenly a loud boom echoed throughout the 1200 building. At first, we believed it to be the computer cart falling over. Mrs. Lippel made us stay quiet, as she must have heard it differently. Soon after, the fire bell went off; hesitantly, students began to flood the halls. I was skeptical since we had already had a drill earlier that day, so I decided to stay by the door.

In the hallway, students stood awaiting evacuation. From the stairwell I heard a sound like that of a wild stampede. Students then began to sprint up the stairwells, shoving one another, screaming as they scrambled to find safety in classrooms. I was pushed to the opposite side of the hallway. Unaware of what was happening, my mind subconsciously entered survival mode.

I was so flustered I couldn't think straight. A teacher told us to return to the other side of the hallway; once back by the door Mrs. Lippel pulled me into the room. I ran in and hid in a large pile of my classmates who were sitting down in the far corner of Mrs. Lippel's room. I will never forget their faces as pure terror and anxiety masked their quirky, imaginative selves. My mind began racing on regrets, death, and never seeing my family again. I felt like a bullet was going to hit me any second. Shaking, I managed to pull out my phone, mute it, and write a text to my immediate family. The text read "I just want you to know I love you all and don't worry, I will be okay."

Even though I had written this, I truly believed I was going to die. The gunshots grew louder, and I shut my eyes and held my hoodie tighter over my head. The worst part then came. Silence overtook the atmosphere, only to be disturbed by the fading screams of the victims crying for help down below. The sound of police soon echoed the halls as help finally arrived after what felt like years.

Once the police entered our room, tears of joy and cheers overtook the fear and intensity. We were then told to look straight up and put our hands over our heads and exit the stairwell. We entered a war zone. Smoke filled the air as rose petals and blood covered the floor. I looked up, as instructed, to see bullet holes and broken windows.

I came out of that building a different person than the one who left for school that day.

Valentine's Day

By Brianna Jesionowski

Valentine's Day,
A day full of love,
Of showing how much you care,
Yet it was the complete opposite,
It was full of screaming,
Of crying in fear,
Of losing our loved ones.

Valentine's Day,
A perfect day,
Or so we thought,
Fourth period holds the memories,
The horror-filled faces,
The sinking of my heart,
The love our teacher held for us,
Valentine's Day,
Will it ever be the same?
I think not.

Photo by Sam Grizelj

In the Life of a Flower

by Daniela Ortiz-Machado

A flower lives just as surely as it dies.
It is not immune to life.
From its humble seed, it grows, and it blossoms,
serving its purpose before it wilts away.

But who's to say what that purpose is.
On Valentine's Day, it should be love.
Love of the purest kind.

On our Valentine's Day,
Desks were littered with carnations, notes of love and friendship
   were read out loud,
In only the purest of voices.
Fingers ran across the stems, their sweet scents of clove and
   vanilla wafted through the air,
And their soft petals brushed up against cheeks.

If every petal was a wish, a smile, a dream, a teardrop, a life,
Then seventeen of those petals would have fallen to the floor.
Our flowers are wilting before serving their purpose,
And no force of nature can possibly explain why.

We watered them, and fed them, and gave them light,
So why is this happening?
Why are they slipping through our fingers, piece by piece?

Seventeen flowers and counting,
And we can't make the wilting stop.
Why won't the wilting stop?

The Day That Changed My Life

by Nadia Murillo

The morning of February 14, I woke up to a pile of Valentine's Day gifts on my dresser from my parents. I got ready for school and wore my favorite red shirt for Valentine's Day. We picked up my best friend from her house and were on our way to school. During the drive, we were making jokes about us having valentines and all the balloons/bears that fellow students were carrying. As we exited the car, I said to my mom, "Bye! Love you!" and blew her a kiss, like I would any other day. Valentine's Day has always been one of my favorite holidays because of all the love and happiness shared on that day. I went to my first period, study hall. In that class I did what I normally would every other day: listen to music, study, and do homework. The bell rang for us to go to second period. I walked to my English 1 Honors class, which was in the 1200 building. My teacher had warned us about a fire drill that we would be having that period, so my class and I headed out to our zone like any other normal fire drill.

Once the drill ended, we headed back to our class and did some *Lord of the Flies* classwork. The bell then rang for third period, which was my Spanish 3 Honors class. I walked to my class on the opposite side of the school. Almost every day, Cara Loughran and I would be the first ones waiting to get into Spanish class. We would usually talk about Spanish homework, tests, quizzes, and other subjects. That day we did our normal Spanish work and went into mini work groups. Little did I know that that would be the last time I would ever see and talk to her. It was time for lunch and I met up with two of my closest friends. We exchanged some Valentine's candy and ate lunch together. We socialized with our friends for a bit, then it was time to head to fourth period, where our lives would forever change.

I headed to my Finance and Business Technology class, which was only a few steps from the 1200 building. The lesson for the day was all about Excel and learning how to use it correctly. I sat right next to the door in that class and had a clear view of the 1200 building. Toward the end of the school day, the girl who sits across from me and I both heard noises, some type of bang, but we didn't think much of it. I thought, "Maybe it was some construction nearby or the janitor going through the closet." The fire alarm went off, and everyone in my class was a bit confused because we'd had one earlier, and we have never had two fire drills in one day. Still, we didn't think much of it. I quickly grabbed my phone because I thought the dismissal bell would ring right after it.

As I was about to take a step outside, I heard the first gunshots that I had ever heard in my life. There were five or six of them. I started to run back into the classroom and said loudly, "I think there's a shooting," to warn my classmates not to go out there. I wasn't sure if it was a drill or a real shooting, as we had talked earlier in the year about having active shooter drills. My teacher started to yell at all the students to get back inside the classrooms. No one really knew if it was a drill or not, but I knew I wasn't going to risk anything, so I did what my instincts told me, and took it as if it were a real shooting. About half of my class had already walked outside. I quickly ran into the closet of my classroom and started to text my mom: "Do we have a drill?" and "We heard gun shots, but it might be a drill let me know what it is." My mom was as confused as I was. She works for the fire department in a nearby city, so she was searching and asking all the firefighters around if they had heard anything about it.

Approximately thirty other classmates, my teacher, and I squeezed inside the closet of the classroom, not knowing what was happening and where the gunshots were coming from. I texted my parents, letting them know what was going on, what I heard, and that I was in a closet with my classmates and my teacher. As the word started to reach social media, it was confirmed that there was an active shooter on campus. My first instinct was to pray. I prayed that the shooter would not come into my class, that all my friends were okay, that my family would stay calm, and that this was not really happening. The thoughts just kept going through my mind: "How could this happen? In such a safe, loving, and caring community, why would someone commit such a horrible act of violence?" Surprisingly, I wasn't crying, but I was shaking a lot and did not talk much. My teacher would leave the closet every few minutes to make sure the door was still locked and to see if she could hear anything going on. My mom just kept texting me not to worry, that it will be okay, and that my father was on his way to school.

As the minutes flew by, the heat started to rise and all of us were sharing cold waters and using paper plates as fans. We didn't hear any more gunshots and there still wasn't any news of the shooter being caught. Many rumors had been spreading around, though, which made me worry even more. Then my mom asked if my best friend had texted me, and in that moment I started to freak out. As I was texting her, her parents texted me asking if I knew what she was wearing that morning, if I had heard from her, and what classroom she would be in. I texted her and never got an answer. Her parents then got ahold of her, and I was so relieved.

After about an hour standing in the closet of my class-room, we heard the door being pushed open and everyone silenced. We heard police radios and a knock on the closet door. My teacher opened the door, and we all took a deep breath and felt a sigh of safety. We started to tear up—we were finally out, and all we wanted to do was hug and kiss our families and friends.

There were three to five SWAT and police officers pointing their guns toward us, telling us to put down our paper plates, leave all our bags there, and run for our lives. They made us go the long way, to avoid any dead bodies and blood outside the 1200 building, only a few steps away from where we were. My class and I ran and ran until we were stopped by other police and told to sit down on the grass in front of our school. I saw one of my close friends, who I had had lunch with earlier that day, and we were just so happy to see each other and know that we were safe. At that moment, everything came together for me and I understood the enormity of what had just occurred. Our biggest fears had just turned into reality. The police then asked us three questions: "Is anyone injured or shot?" "Did anyone see the shooter?" "Did anyone capture pictures/videos of the shooter or shooting?"

Quickly after, we were told to go to the other side of the road, where I called my dad. He was waiting at the school for me, and he told me where to go to meet up with him. He also let me know that my best friend was okay and that her phone was still inside her classroom in the 1200 building, which made sense. I quickly rushed to my dad and gave him a hug and kiss, which is when I started crying nonstop, because when I was hiding in the closet, all I wanted to do was hug my parents and sister.

He drove as fast as he could to my best friend's house, so we could see each other. Right when I stepped into her house, the waterworks began again. I hugged her as tightly as I could, and I hugged my little sister tighter than I ever had as we both cried. I hugged my best friend's mother, father, and sisters, who are like family to me. My mom then walked in the door and that was the best moment ever. We both cried, said "I love you," and hugged tightly for a long time. She had helped me stay calm throughout the shooting and told me everything was going to be all right. I was crying nonstop for the rest of the night. My friends and I started communicating and making sure we were okay. Videos popped up of the footage students had captured, photos of missing students began appearing on my social media, and texts from family members and friends kept coming once they heard what happened from the media. I finally went home and gave my grandparents a hug and a kiss. I needed to take a shower and calm down before I went to bed. I wanted to make sure the news was on the TV at all times, in case any information was announced. That night we knew very little about the fatalities and injuries, but we did find out who the shooter was. Having to see his face and know that he did something so terrible to my school and community took all our innocence and made me feel so unsafe in the place I had always felt secure from any type of danger.

That night I slept in bed with my parents and little sister. I didn't want to ever let go. I only slept for about four hours. It took a long time before I was able to fall asleep, and I would wake up at random times during the night. In the morning, I would learn that two of my beautiful

Illustration by Isabella Pfeiffer

friends, Cara and Jaime, had been killed, as well as fifteen other people. Later that morning my best friend's family and my family went to therapy at a nearby community center. We talked, we cried, and we laughed. It was good to talk to someone. But after that was one of the saddest events that I would ever be a part of, a candlelight vigil held at a nearby park. At the center stage of the vigil, seventeen angel statues were lit up to represent the seventeen lives taken the day before. We all cried and held each other close as we remembered the Eagles we had lost. Seeing the MSD community come together was so inspiring. Knowing that we had so many people who loved us gave us hope and comfort.

The days after that were similar—filled with crying and being with friends for comfort. We also attended Cara's candlelight vigil and funerals for our friends. A week after the tragedy, I had the opportunity to have an interview with CNN on my views on the gun laws, what I went through during the shooting, and what I would say to politicians. Many students also went to Tallahassee for the #NeverAgain rally to protest current gun laws. Around the same time, the March For Our Lives was announced. Student activists from my school started the march to motivate politicians to rethink their views on gun control and how to make our schools safer. I attended the March For Our Lives in Parkland. Hearing so many motivational speeches and seeing so many people show up to this movement really demonstrates how much we are cared for.

This whole experience has made me look at things differently. I will not take anything for granted, and I will always watch my surroundings. I will forever miss my talks with Cara and Jaime. Everything we do now is for our seventeen angels.

Proud to Be an Eagle
BY SARA LESMES

I was sitting in my class, ready to go
The fire alarm sounded but our teacher told us no
The kids didn't listen, instead they went out
But then we all became filled with doubt

Then someone came on the intercom
Alerting us of a shooter and deadly smoke bombs
The kids around me thought it was a drill
But I knew it was a man with motive to kill

I ran to the corner of our small classroom
As soon as I crouched, all I heard was a boom
But then one became two, and two became five
And the next thing you know, we feared for our lives

I sat in a corner, five boys by my side
There weren't many places for us to hide
He could open the door and see us there
All huddled in a corner, wide eyed in fear

Two hours later, we heard a sound
It was the police and we were finally found
I left the school, hands over my head
"It's over, it's over," the police had said

I finally went home and turned on the news
And the one to blame is Nikolas Cruz
He's the one who took seventeen
With a weapon of war, an AR-15

Illustration by Isabella Pfeiffer

FEBRUARY 14, 2018

by Sarah Lerner, English and journalism teacher at MSD

Valentine's Day started out as a normal Wednesday. I was giving a quiz to my senior English classes on book one of *1984* by George Orwell. As they took their quiz, I dropped Hershey Kisses on their desks. I wore leggings with hearts on them. I received gifts and flowers from some students. It really was a good day.

I was working on some yearbook pages when the fire alarm went off during fourth period. I looked at the clock. It was 2:20. I took my class outside. That's when I heard the popping sounds. I turned around, heading back toward the staircase to lead me up to my classroom in Building 6. I saw my class scatter like cockroaches. I ended up with five of my students, and ten from the teacher next door. From my doorway, I could clearly see Building 12. I had no idea what was happening within those four walls.

I got the kids in, locked the door. We sat, unsure of what was going on. My computers were on my desk across the room. All I had with me was my phone and keys. Among the students in my room were the senior class salutatorian

Photo by Sarah Lerner

and valedictorian. I texted in my English teacher group chat with four friends to ask what was going on. It was 2:27. That's when the texts began flooding in.

I told my husband and mom that there was an active shooter on campus. My son texted me from the middle school next door that he was on lockdown. I told all three of them that I was okay. I wasn't shot. I had an out-of-body experience with that, because what mother, wife, daughter should ever have to say that? I found out shortly after 2:35 that one of my teacher friends had been shot (we later found out that she had been grazed). I also received a text that one of my yearbook photographers had been shot (she later said that she had been grazed).

Thoughts ran through my head. How would I cover this in the yearbook? What if this had been the next day? The last period of the day was when I had yearbook . . . how many students would I have lost? Where did my seniors from English end up? Are my friends safe? What's really going on? How long will I be in my classroom?

At around 5:30, the SWAT team released us from the room. I had to identify myself as the classroom teacher. We walked out with our hands over our heads. We serpentined to get off campus and waited. Waited to be reunited with friends. Waited to see parents, siblings, spouses, children. Waited to be transported to the next location. Waited to hear what actually happened. Waited to hear who didn't make it.

Over the next few hours, I would find out the fate of those in the 1200 building. I lost Meadow and Jaime, two of my students; I had Meadow in my English class when she was a freshman, and I had Jaime this year in my Journalism I class. I lost Chris Hixon, a friend who spent hours year after year to help make sure I had everything I needed for the sports pages in the yearbook. I lost Aaron Feis, who would take my son to school next door in his golf cart when it was raining.

I lost so much more. I lost my sense of safety. I lost my sense of innocence. I lost my sense of security. I lost my ability to see the world as I had only hours earlier. I would give anything to go back to the way things were before the fire alarm rang. I know that I can't. What I can do is use my voice and work hard for the rest of my life to make change— change that will create a better, safer world for my children.

I lost so much, but we all lost seventeen Eagles that day. They now fly high above us, protecting us, encouraging us to make this world a better place. We work hard for them. We are positive. We are passionate. We are proud to be Eagles. We are MSD Strong.

I sit in my room, with my best friend,
    moments after escaping the end.
We watch the news flash by, images of
    moments before.
We listen to names. Rumors float by.
    Of those who left us, I want to cry.
17 of my own. Eagles gone.
The sounds ensue. A dreadful song.
I do not believe in heaven. But I hope
    I am wrong.

by Ryan Servaites

They sit in their suits, earmuffs block
    out our pleas.
We ask and we scream, and we get on
    our knees.
What will it take for something to change?
You could have stopped this.
Now help us stop the pain.
We know what it brings.
But you seem to care more about your
    "toys" than our future.
So we beg, we scream, and we
    plead and cry.
How many more have to die?

by Ryan Servaites

Can't You Hear?
by Alyson Sheehy

I have only been on this planet for eighteen years
And yet I've seen things that should've been stopped
    two decades ago.
Not even born and shots fill other high schoolers' ears
But that happened twenty years ago.

Once more, sitting at a desk similar to the ones in
    Newtown,
Not knowing what was happening nineteen hours
    away.
They were left riddled with holes and flipped upside
    down
And twenty-six lives were taken away.

Now I find myself on the floor covering my ears
First in denial, but then the screams.
Lives were taken, and made his souvenirs
But you didn't hear the screams.
Can't you hear the screams now
Can't you hear
Can't you hear
Can't you hear us scream now?

Lists of names appear and leave families broken
Left to pick up the pieces from their empty lives.

Shouts of pain replace the words left unspoken
Enough. It's too many lives.

People send their thoughts and prayers
Denying the actual cause and telling us it isn't
    the time.
Yet their thoughts and prayers and tweets and shares
Will not decrease the number dead the next time.

This has become a new normal, and it's insanity
Because the numbers rise and dates grow closer
    together.
Politicians turn to dollar signs instead of basic
    humanity
And constantly divide, all the while claiming they're
    working together.
Can't you hear the screams now
Can't you hear
Can't you hear
Can't you hear us scream now?

Our lives are forever defined by that day.
You may see a smile, but that doesn't mean we're not
    hurting.
We are done with the people we love being ripped
    away.
I am done with this stupid thing that causes all this
    hurting.

We've had to take the matter into our own hands

Dealing with the blame and the constant fear of it
	happening again.
Our voices will not be words lost to the shifting sands
For when November comes, we won't let them forget
	again.

You can blame what you want, pull on whatever thread
Bully us into silence and treat us like we don't matter.
However, don't forget there is no future when all of us
	are dead
Although it seems that is still not enough for all lives
	to matter.

Can't you hear the screams now? Cause they are only
	growing louder.

Photo by Natasha Martinez

Rainbow*

Presented on February 14, third period

BY HAYDEN KORR

I've been searching for the perfect shade of love,
something that feels like the color lavender and the
    smell of peaches,
something that reminds me of pink ice cream on
    beaches.
It doesn't exist here, between us, that kind of colorful
    love, well, sort of,
since love isn't warm tones, and love isn't easy, and
    love especially isn't a gift from above.
If it were love, I'd race down green hills to match the
    speed of my heart. No, it isn't in pieces.
If it were perfect, it wouldn't be this, it wouldn't be
    mocha-eyed stares that leave me speechless.
It's not the vermilion pangs in my chest and it's not us
    alone, it's not a sky full of white doves.

Maybe, love doesn't have to be perfectly blue, it only
    truly has to be with you.
Maybe, it can be a hurricane of senses, maybe, it can
    be messy and green.
Yes, it's close to love, I feel it when you're near and the
    yellows burst in my chest,

when time escapes me; when my mean reds turn into
    softer hues.
This tint of love is vivid and bright; it is brilliantly
    liberating and it is violently clean.
I believe this could be the perfect shade of love,
    something rainbow at best.

*This piece was presented and read aloud on
February 14, during Hayden's third-period
AP Literature and Composition class.*

Black Bullets

Written on February 17
as a follow-up to "Rainbow"

BY HAYDEN KORR

February 14, 2018
A day that was intended to be bursting at the seams
    with red hearts and pink flowers
A day where affection was supposed to be received in
    shining showers
On February 14, 2018, I was searching for the perfect
    shade of love, something that would glow and
    gleam
My biggest concerns being my dinner plans and the
    endless amount of chocolates and everything in
    between
Ever since that day, our world has been soaked in
    blues and greens turned sour
Every hour a battle between my grief and willpower
The same monochrome scenes playing over and over
    and over and over, the same sirens and the same
    screams and the same bleak scenery as I ran and
    ran and ran, white surrounding me with no sign of
    stopping.
Would you stop if you knew?
if you knew the vermilions we experienced that day,
the blacks our lives shifted to?

if you had to pray for the first time in your life, when
    your friend never responded to you?
if you went to vigil after vigil after funeral after
    funeral, the rainbow that encompassed you fading
    to gray?
Somehow, through the darkness, we found another
    shade of love, too
something that outweighed the hate and swept the
    grays away.
A love so strong it transcended colors, something so
    empowering and true it couldn't be traced to one
    hue.

February 14, 2018, the day my world was built anew.
A world without 17 eagles soaring away
But a world built stronger and kinder
A world where strangers tell us, we love you
A world that we'll manage, despite it all, anyway
A world with a few different colors, burning vibrant
    and lighter

The Dying Rose
by Alexis Gendron

The dying rose has but two emotions
Sadness & Anger
The dying rose does not wish to feel
 these emotions, but it does.
It is beautiful, yet horrible
 to look at,
Horrible because something so beautiful
 is dying.
The dying rose loses a petal each day
Because it has been hurt so many times.
Hurt by a boy who hated his life & ended
 17 others just to feel better
Hurt by the media that refuses to show
 what is really happening to the rose
Hurt by the people who lie to earn fame
 out of this rose's suffering.
The dying rose was once full of
 life & happiness
Until that Valentine's Day.
The rose assumed that day would
 be perfect for sharing love
But it became a day of pain & sadness.
Now the dying rose loses a petal
 every day
Seeming to fade away
Not knowing how much more it can take.

Like me.
I'm losing more and more of myself
   each day
I'm seeming to fade away
I don't know how much more I can take.

Photo by Kyra Parrow

Through My Eyes
by Aly Peri

Through my eyes,
I see the crowded halls,
I see the painful smiles
and the lost souls.

Through my eyes,
I can picture the hurt,
the broken
and everything after that.

Through my eyes,
I watch all the fearful teens
cry and sob to their loved ones
and try to cover it with a faint smile.

Through my eyes,
I look at all the dreams washed away.
But that's just through _my_ eyes.

No Normal Day
by Taylor Ferrante-Markham

February 14, 2018, known as the international day of love, started as a normal school day for the students of Marjory Stoneman Douglas High School, until 2:30 rolled around and our lives were changed forever.

Fourth period was about to end, and the students and faculty were getting ready to go home. But instead of hearing the dismissal bell, everyone soon heard the second fire alarm of the day, which spurred an immense amount of confusion. My classroom was in the back portion of campus, and I evacuated with my class and waited for Principal Thompson to come on the loudspeaker to announce it was a mistake, or that culinary had burnt something. That announcement never came. Instead, I heard four faint pops, then saw a teacher I knew running with his class—down the stairs and onto the field where we were standing. I turned to my best friend, Grace, and she asked me if I heard what she just did. I told her that it had to be something else, anything else, though we both suspected what those faint pops were. The next thing we heard was our teacher yelling at us to run.

Following the evacuation route was a slow walk behind our campus and the middle school campus located next to Stoneman Douglas. People's minds started filling with confusion that changed to panic as we were hearing there was an active shooter in the Freshman Building and that people were hurt and passing away. I texted the people I'm in a group chat with and we all responded saying we were okay. I texted my mom telling her what was happening and that I loved her. She then called me and informed me the shooter was "at large," meaning he could be anywhere. I was worried I would be next. I called two of my close friends, Michael and Jordan, and they both told me they were still on campus on lockdown, and I broke down in tears.

The thought of two of my best friends stuck in there and the possibility of them getting hurt was too painful. After walking single file up the canal onto Holmberg Road, I found my mom. She was rushing me and Grace to get back to the Walmart parking lot, where she'd left her car because of all the traffic congestion in the area. I saw my friend's brother in the parking lot and made him stay by my side until I could get him to his sister, who was in the Freshman Building on the first floor. I was determined to make sure he was okay and that he got to his family. I wouldn't leave him alone in that moment. We waited together until his parents told him to go to a close friend's house. Then Grace, my mom, and I left Walmart and started heading to my house. Driving there was like landing in the middle of a scene of *Criminal Minds*. We must've passed at least twenty cop cars on the five-minute journey, which at the time confused me because none of us had any idea what was going on. We later found out the police were heading in that direction to catch and arrest the shooter, who was in the area of my apartment building complex.

During the car ride I was replying to dozens of texts from my family members and friends checking in to see if I was okay. That's when I first heard the suspected shooter's name. Grace and I ran into my room the minute we pulled in the driveway, turned on the news to get some insight on what was happening, and ripped open last year's yearbook trying to find the shooter. When we found his picture in the book, we immediately sent it to our friends to let them know to be on the lookout. Then we tried to locate people who had not gotten in contact with their families or who had never come home that day. They were reported missing and had their pictures plastered all over social media.

That day, two lists were made, one for the found and injured and another for the found who had passed. Seventeen names were added to each list. February 14 is a day nobody would forget—not the people who attend Stoneman Douglas, not the people who live in the surrounding area, and not even people across the country. The students assembled a movement that became known internationally. Now writing this three months later, it feels as if time has stood still. We all take life day by day and try to do our best to make it through each one while we practice our methods of coping. My way of coping was heading down to the tattoo shop and forever memorializing the victims with the word "love" and a number 17 connected to it.

One thing we as survivors can prove is that love overcomes hate, and we will continue to fight, for our seventeen injured and our seventeen angels. That's a promise.

Cassie • Daniel • Steve • Daniel • Corey
Sanders • Matt • John • Charlotte • Em
Ana • Dylan • Hochsprung • madeleine •
Grace • Murphy • Jack • Noah • carolin
Sherlach • Soto • Benjamin • Allison •
Austin • Jocelyne • Kevin •
Rachel • Emily • Jarrett •
Partahi • Lauren • Daniel •
Julia • Mary • Reema • Waleed •
Thomas • Robert • Thomas •
Claudia • Billy • Edna •
Sarena • Lawrence •
Kim • Treven • Jeff •
michelle • Neva
Chanelle •
Sonam •
• David

Carmen • Meadow • Peter • Nicholas
Martin • Alyssa • Helena • Beigel • Jo

Illustration by Alyson Sheehy

achel • Kelly • Isaiah • Lauren • Kyle •
• Daniel • Davino • Olivia • Josephine •
therine • chase • Jesse • James •
Jessica • Avielle • Rousseau •
Ross • christopher • Brian • Ryan •
Matthew • caitlin • Jeremy •
Henry • Matthew • Liviu • G.V. •
Juan • Minal • Daniel • Erin • Mike
Leselie • Maxine • Nicole • Roy •
Martin • Karen • David • Thomas
Harry • Kathy • Margaret •
Lucas • Quinn • Jason • Lucero
Alcaraz • Rebecka • Daryl •
• Derrick • Alicia • Thuriene •
chase • Dewayne • Doris •
Katie • chris • George • James
• veronika • scott ♥

ixon • Feis • Luke • Alaina • Jaime •
in • Cara • Gina • Alexander • ♥

NEVER AGAIN
by Lyliah Skinner

When you hear it, it doesn't seem like much
It's hard to visualize 17 bodies, all cold to touch
It's a lot to take in, you don't truly realize
17 innocent people, never again can open their eyes

Never again

To some, it's just a trending Twitter phrase
But for me, it moves and guides me in all types
    of ways
To me, it's a promise, a glowing red warning
BECAUSE ALL HUMAN BEINGS DESERVE TO
    SEE THE NEXT MORNING

I still haven't gotten closure
Especially with the constant and overwhelming
    exposure

I see you in everything
In sunlight, lyrics, and flowers
As your names cross my mind every second
    of every hour

Dear Angels, I hope that you're all together
My love for you will go on forever and ever

My Story

(By Brianna Jesionowski)

Confusion clouds my mind,
Didn't know I could be so blind,
As the shots filled the room,
The atmosphere was gloom,
Thinking that it was a drill,
I didn't realize later I'd feel ill,
Watching as the smoke fills the halls,
I consult my friend as she bawls,
It's past time to leave,
Didn't think that soon I'd have to grieve,
Hearing the yelling outside,
I was left red-eyed,
As the window shatters,
We realize it's not a laughing matter,
Questions asked as we get checked,
Looking in the halls it's all wrecked,
The events of Valentine's Day
Have left me Gray.

2/14/18: The Day My Whole Life Changed
by Kaleela Rosenthal

Another fire drill, another reason to leave class early.

As I pack up, I see the only two girls I knew in my study hall, Jaime and Cara. Usually we would walk together at the end of the day, but today, my priority was getting home.

"I'll see them next class, no big deal."

I stroll down the hall following a group of familiar boys from my class until we were put to a permanent stop.

At that moment, I was pulled into a classroom by the fear of being trampled by running students.

Confusion clouded my mind. "Is this some Valentine's Day joke?"

Moments after I entered that classroom,

Shots started ringing.

The whole classroom became dense with fear. . . . I will never forget that feeling of uncertainty.

The only thing I wanted was to stay home in my own bubble and reflect.

Reflect on what I had just gone through.

Through bloody hallways, slumped-over corpses, and air filled with the stench of gunpowder.

At that moment, all I wanted was to know my friends were "okay."

Once the night progressed, "missing" posts were scattered all over.

My face turned pale at the sight of my friend Gina, missing.

At that moment "okay" meant that she was injured and unconscious in the hospital . . . that is what I wished . . . that qualified as okay.

I would soon realize that "missing" was a death sentence.

That night consisted of blank expressions and calming my friends down. It hadn't hit me yet.

The next morning was filled with the aching feeling of wanting to be with friends.

We watched together as the names were released, and we hoped that we wouldn't hear her name. "Gina Montalto . . ." We just sat there, silent. Some part of us already knew she passed. We continued listening, and through the sobs of tears, that's when I heard two more names I didn't want to hear, Jaime and Cara.

That's when I realized . . . I left them in that building.

Uncertainties in the Aftermath

by Samantha Bonnin

I don't know if my poetry is healing
I don't know if it's meant to wipe away the blood
   of seventeen brutal murders
I don't know if it's even meant to quiet my
   discontented soul,
If it's meant to bring me acceptance
Or if it's even meant to allow me to acknowledge
   this entire ordeal
This entire mess,
To wrap my fragile mind around
The fact that my school became a mass graveyard
   in a matter of minutes
The fact that I'll never hear her voice again and all her
   sarcasm
The fact that he aimed to kill
That he aimed to bathe the hallways in a sea of red

I don't know if I can ever come to comprehend this
How one day I was stressing about scattered feelings
   of high school love
And the next I said "I love you" so many times that
The mere phrase has seemed to connect with all the
   other words in my vocabulary

I just don't want to let go of all the people I love,
I want to continuously tell them "I love you" until
My voice is raw and my throat is sore
And I want to hug them with such a crushing embrace
That I can make the pain of this break and give way
To the world realigning to okay again

Photo by Kyra Parrow

First Night
By Brianna Jesionowski

My eyes won't close,
I'm staring at the ceiling,
My thoughts are so slow,
Don't know what I'm feeling,
Did this really happen,
It wasn't a drill,
Please don't make this a habit,
How many did he kill,
After hours of no sleep,
My eyes slip shut,
As I still weep,
There's a feeling in my gut,
I wake up screaming,
The memories haunt my head,
The tears keep streaming,
I feel brain dead,
No sleep came again.

Journal Entry — February 15, 2018

by Chantal Chalita

I'm just an average girl going to a random school that probably most of the country never knew until now. 99.999 percent of this world's population doesn't know me; I'm insignificant to them and their lives. For everyone watching the national news and observing the shooting from afar, it sounds horrible but it also sounds far away and unrealistic, something that could only happen in movies. It seems as though to you, yet another average person, the chances of this happening, well, would not be high. I never thought this would happen here in my community.

Parkland is a bubble, and it is a safe bubble. My friends and I have always joked about this, how in Parkland nothing from the real world ever happens. But right now this average girl at this random school has lost classmates and a best friend who did not deserve to die. This has all been so hard to process, but to those readers out there, let this be a lesson that we as a country must do something and speak out. Don't let all these casualties and injuries, traumatizing moments in the lives of every single student and their families, be in vain.

Photo by Suzanna Barna

We Call BS speech

by Emma González

These are excerpts from the speech Emma González gave at the Fort Lauderdale rally on February 17, 2018.

Every single person up here today, all these people should be home grieving. But instead we are up here standing together because if all our government and President can do is send "thoughts and prayers," then it's time for victims to be the change that we need to see. Since the time of the Founding Fathers and since they added the Second Amendment to the Constitution, our guns have developed at a rate that leaves me dizzy. The guns have changed but our laws have not. We certainly do not understand why it should be harder to make plans with friends on weekends than to buy an automatic or semi-automatic weapon. In Florida, to buy a gun you do not need a permit, you do not need a gun license, and once you buy it you do not need to register it. You do not need a permit to carry a concealed rifle or shotgun. You can buy as many guns as you want at one time. . . .

Instead of worrying about our AP Gov chapter 16 test, we

have to be studying our notes to make sure that our arguments based on politics and political history are watertight. The students at this school have been having debates on guns for what feels like our entire lives. AP Gov had about three debates this year. Some discussions on the subject even occurred during the shooting while students were hiding in the closets. The people involved right now, those who were there, those posting, those tweeting, those doing interviews and talking to people, are being listened to for what feels like the very first time on this topic that has come up over 1,000 times in the past four years alone. . . .

I watched an interview this morning and noticed that one of the questions was, do you think your children will have to go through other school shooter drills? And our response is that our neighbors will not have to go through other school shooter drills when we've had our say with the government. And maybe the adults have gotten used to saying "it is what it is," but if us students have learned anything, it's that if you don't study, you will fail. And in this case if you actively do nothing, people continually end up dead, so it's time to start doing something.

We are going to be the kids you read about in textbooks. Not because we're going to be another statistic about mass shooting in America, but because, just as David said, we are going to be the last mass shooting. Just like *Tinker v. Des Moines*, we are going to change the law. That's going to be Marjory Stoneman Douglas in that textbook and it's going to be due to the tireless effort of the school board, the faculty members, the family members and most of all the students. . . .

If the President wants to come up to me and tell me to my face that it was a terrible tragedy and how it should never have happened and maintain telling us how nothing is going to be done about it, I'm going to happily ask him how much money he received from the National Rifle Association. You want to know something? It doesn't matter, because I already know. Thirty million dollars. And divided by the number of gunshot victims in the United States in the one and one-half months in 2018 alone, that comes out to being $5,800. Is that how much these people are worth to you, Trump? If you don't do anything to prevent this from continuing to occur, that number of gunshot victims will go up and the number that they are worth will go down and we will be worthless to you. To every politician who is taking donations from the NRA, shame on you. . . .

The people in the government who were voted into power are lying to us. And us kids seem to be the only ones who notice and are prepared to call BS.

Companies trying to make caricatures of the teenagers these days, saying that all we are is self-involved and trend-obsessed and they hush us into submission so our message doesn't reach the ears of the nation, we are prepared to call BS.

Politicians who sit in their gilded House and Senate seats funded by the NRA telling us nothing could have been done to prevent this, we call BS.

They say that tougher gun laws do not decrease gun violence. We call BS.

They say a good guy with a gun stops a bad guy with a gun. We call BS.

They say guns are just tools like knives and are as dangerous as cars. We call BS.

They say no laws could have prevented the hundreds of senseless tragedies that have occurred. We call BS.

That us kids don't know what we're talking about, that we're too young to understand how the government works. We call BS.

Photo by Suzanna Barna

Life's Test

By Brianna Jesionowski

Life has a funny way of testing you,
For most it's losing a job,
Getting your heart broken,
Or going bankrupt,
For us it was much worse,
It was watching your friends die,
Listening to the heart-wrenching screams,
Praying for your life,
Seeing blood and dead bodies.
Ours wasn't just a test,
It was the beginning,
The beginning to change our world,
To keep it safe,
To make sure we protect the ones we love,
Our test was really our final.

Photo by Rain Valladares

Kids die, mothers cry
Blood covers the school floor.

Politicians lie, school boards deny
And then it happens once more.

Expect some change
Tired of asking not to die.

by Alyson Sheehy

MY FIRST DAY BACK
by Alejandro Rodriguez

My first day back was a blur. Coming out of the junior lot and seeing the news reporters walking toward us with cameras, lights, and tape recorders, asking us how we felt and what we experienced, was frazzling. As a fifteen-year-old, you really don't expect to be questioned and bombarded like a politician or a celebrity. And seeing all of the policemen outside the bus loop wearing MSD Strong hats and patting us on the back was almost like a boost for me, a little vote of confidence telling me I can get through this. You want to talk to your friends and tell them what you just experienced coming to school—and one of them is no longer there. You wish this could be a normal day at your school, students running around and laughing, talking to each other, but all you see are your fellow students mourning over what happened. Having to find my new fourth-period classroom on my first day back was a little confusing and yet refreshing, because I didn't want to reenter the 1200 building, and it gave me a tiny bit of excitement to see what my new classroom would be like. Then you see your friends' faces and your teacher and you realize you're back where you left off. Wednesday, fourth period. I hug all of my teachers and my friends, so happy to see them. Getting to spend the rest of the period with them makes me forget what happened for a split second. That is, until you see a close friend who has lost a sister, a brother, a girlfriend, or a boyfriend. It's almost like the whole world has sucked the life out of you, and you see and feel a portion of their pain.

Reclaim the Nest
BY DANIELLE RITTMAN

The time period between Valentine's Day and February 28 felt like a blur. All I vividly remember was crying. It was two weeks of support groups, vigils, and crying—a lot of crying. I felt empty. I didn't know what to do with myself. All I could think was "This is not real. . . . This couldn't have happened." I wanted to go back to school. I wanted to go back to dance class. I wanted something that felt normal. But nothing felt normal. I wouldn't see the same people I saw every day in the hallway, and I wouldn't see Jaime's smile when I got to dance at 7:30 on Wednesdays.

We returned to school two weeks after. It was time for us to "reclaim the nest." I remember I woke up extra early that day because I knew it would be difficult to get ready. Though going back gave us a sense of normalcy, it also meant we had to face the fact that this happened at our school. I drove to school with both of my parents that day. There were inspirational banners and signs that said MSD Strong sent by schools all over the country to show their support.

I remember sitting in the drop-off line in the backseat of my mom's car, looking out at hundreds of police officers, therapy dogs, horses, goats, and other animals. My old middle school teachers were there as well. I'll never forget waving, with an empty look on my face, to my favorite teacher from eighth grade. She looked back over her shoulder, faced away from my car, and started crying. She didn't want me to see her cry, but I did, and I started crying, too. Still with tears in my eyes, our car entered the school and I was given a flower from an administrator to welcome me back. I met up with some of my friends before class. We stood outside the cafeteria and petted some of the therapy dogs. Eventually the bell rang, and we picked up exactly where we left off, fourth period, on a Wednesday.

I made cookies for all of my classes for that first day back. I needed to do something the night before to occupy myself, so I baked. I figured bringing in something like cookies could make me feel like I was helping my classmates and myself heal in a small way.

The first day back was very healing, more healing than I thought it would be. We petted dogs, ate snacks, played card games, and talked. For a minute we would feel like normal kids. For many of us, the dogs were our motivation to go to school at first. We just sat at school and petted dogs like we were little kids again.

In my fourth-period English class, we sat and made a list of our class's "new normal." There would be beanbags, picnics, movies, and all the activities that would contribute to our healing process. In my AP World History class, my teacher gave us candy and board games to play, and hung inspirational letters and posters that were sent to our class from around the world. In my yearbook class we discussed how we would cover what had happened, how we would not let this event define the yearbook we had worked so hard to make special. In all of my classes, my teachers spoke kind words and explained how everyone heals differently and it will take time to recover from what we had experienced.

Eventually the school day ended, and I took the bus home, just like normal. The first day back was the first big step in healing for me. It was difficult for the school to handle the return of students, but they did it well. Though it continued to be hard, I looked forward to the next day of school because I knew that when I got home that day, I would have healed a little bit more.

Therapy Dogs

BY ALYSSA MARRERO

When we got back to school and I saw there were therapy dogs on campus, I was ecstatic! Whenever I had a class with a dog in it, I would pet it all period long. Petting the dogs made the day go by so much faster. They were so cute and playful, it was hard to NOT play with them.

One day while leaving school, I walked pass the courtyard and I saw all the golden retrievers huddled in a circle. It was as if they were a doggie gang of golden retrievers trying to intimidate the other dogs! Once spring break came around, I was sad that they were going to be gone. When we got back, however, there were still dogs! While many had left, there were still enough. Even just petting them for a second while I passed them in the hallway made me feel better.

Once fourth quarter started, it felt more exhausting to go to school. It wasn't even because of the work, but just physically coming to the school wore me out. The dogs were one of the main reasons I actually wanted to go to school. They took some weight off my shoulders. I'm going to miss them next school year. My hope is they will, at least, be there the first day of school. I want them to stay at school until all the students who experienced that terrible day graduate, but I know they probably can't.

I am constantly reminded about what happened on February 14. It's always on my mind, but I can honestly say that the dogs were able to take it off my mind, even for just a second. I want to say thank you to the people who brought the therapy dogs—especially those handlers and dogs who came every single day. They took the time to help us feel better. They could have stopped coming after spring break, but they wanted to come back, and it made the rest of the year more bearable.

Breaking Silence
BY ALYSON SHEEHY

I don't like silence anymore.
It used to be a palace,
A place I could hide from the world,
But now that's gone.
Like so much in my life,
My palace has turned upside down.
Instead I'm constantly falling,
Farther and farther,
Not knowing where the bottom is
Or when it will stop.
A constant buzz passes my ears
As images replay in front of my eyes
And the what-if's
Cut into my soul like daggers.
No matter how hard I try
Silence likes to follow me
And take over my thoughts.
It's not the same silence I used to cherish.
Now he has taken a new name
And his face haunts
Taunting the deepest parts of my mind
Not letting go.
Ripping apart what once was

And leaving a trail of shredded memories.
A palace I saw as sacred
Has been desecrated by him.
I sit and try to drown him out,
Only to be sucked back in
To the never-ending abyss
He has carved meticulously into the quietness.
Silence, my old friend,
I should be happy that I have a chance
A chance to make a difference
To make a change
So tell that imposter that dares
To force the darkness onto everything
That I am done.
I want my palace back.

I want you here
I know
I know
I know you are here
But it's only in spirit
And that's not enough
I spend nights
Wishing to see your smiles
Hear your laughs
Just one last time
My heart hurts
Looking at the emptiness
That has been left behind
I don't know what to do

I don't know
I don't know
I don't know if any of this is right
Walking has changed
Breathing is different
I feel guilty
You're gone
Yet I'm still here
And that just feels wrong
There's so much left
So much to do
But you don't get the chance
To even try
As if we knew
As if we knew
As if we knew this could happen
I'm glad I said see you later
Instead of goodbye
Cause it's true
I'll see you, when I join you
Only it might take a while
And that hurts too
I guess
I just
Really
Miss you.

Photo by Sam Grizelj

puppy therapy: misty
by Samantha Deitsch

so much joy in something so small
my puppy misty, the best medicine of all
she's energetic, loving, and fun
and super sweet to everyone
the tears disappear
when her kisses get near
always ready to play
or cuddle on a bad day
she brings so much healing by being herself
bringing the community mental health
i love her so much that she's been spoiled
the light of our lives, the darkness is foiled

Photo by Samantha Deitsch

ADD
by Augustus Griffith Jr.

I'm pleading for peace and I just need a reason to
    let you go.

I'm afraid of the future.
Life is moving too fast
Honor roll, college essays and I just peer through
    the glass
Everything I meant a moment ago is in the past
Won't you hold my hand and never let go?
Won't you never leave because with me,
    you're special?
You're simply too unique to me
You can amaze so easily,
I hope you believe in me
I got a bad case of ADD

I remember when reality was boring and not
    painful, distorted.
Pain is for people who can't get out of bed
    in the morning.

I'm no survivor, I would've never made it
    in your shoes
And I guess I'll never find out who
Knocked on the door, 1250-something, pleading
    for life
I'm just lucky, cause I shouldn't be alive
Sleep is the cousin of death
Sleep is my only escape
Hopefully I come back, hopefully I don't change
Brimming with feelings I still can't avoid
I'm filling a void

Your pain is like you, deceiving
We're the same, so I'm leaving
I don't know what you see in me
You love me, you hate me, you don't
We hurt each other so easily
I hope you call back, but you won't
I don't call myself innocent, I betray the trust that
    we share
Sometimes you need me and I'm not there
Or I just don't care
Because I'm burning my bridges
I don't care for religion, been to too many vigils
Don't give a damn if you miss me,
I'm gone.

I hope you believe in me
Swear you'll never leave me

It's my ADD,
Lately don't feel up for anything
Why would they take you instead of me?
How did one monster kill seventeen?
I see the sights when I close my eyes
Everything's red, but the world was our canvas
Walk on by, there's a crime scene on campus
On their last legs, teachers cross names off
    of rosters
Students crying over empty desks cause we
    lost her
Boys, men and women alike respond to a cry
    for activism
I open my mouth to speak, but no words
    come out.

All Over Again
by Caitlynn Tibbetts

Cameras.

Interviewers.

Microphones.

To think I was simply hurrying down a sidewalk, my two friends on either side of me, nerves racking my entire body. My feet moved of their own accord. My hands shook as the boy beside me explained to a cameraman following us that he was simply happy to be back and begin the healing process. I was just walking to school from the parking lot, but the ten-minute journey there felt like I was on the set of a movie, and I was just another extra in the background of an important scene. It just so happened to be a crime scene.

Roses.

Hugs.

Posters.

The support was overwhelming. Suffocating. Every time I inhaled there was someone handing me a gift, their words thrown in my face or shoved down my throat. Love was finally tangible, love was finally something I could hold in my hands.

My arms were filled with play dough, bears, flowers, stress balls, coloring book pages. Therapy dogs roamed the hallways with their respective owners, students throwing themselves at them, excited to pet the happy animals. We all just wanted to be happy again, and we would take it back in any form that we could.

Tears.

Silence.

Darkness.

What is strength? Was it shown there that day? I do not know. My teachers cried harder than I thought an adult could, angry that children had to experience something of this magnitude. My classmates and I felt the empty spot in our room, a vacant chair that should have been filled.

As I left campus that day, earlier than usual, of course, because how could I be there for longer than a few hours, I felt the wave of guilt crash over me. I got to go back. Seventeen others did not. I have the chance to live my life, to heal. Seventeen others do not.

Photo by Rain Valladares

Journal Entry #1

BY JACK MACLEOD

On February 14, 2018, I woke up to a regular school day, ready for love. Not only was it Valentine's Day, but Ash Wednesday as well. It was a day of community, unity, and togetherness. Little did I know it wouldn't stay like that.

As I strolled through campus to my first period, I walked alongside the Freshman Building. I remembered when I had classes in there. I remembered the classrooms I sat in, the subjects I learned, and the people I met. This was nothing more than a passing thought. Nothing of importance to me, at the time anyway.

My first period was casual, as was my second and my third. Balloons floated through the hallways, filled with people whose foreheads were marked with ash. "Quite the day," I thought. Two different cultures clashing together, it was quite beautiful.

Besides that, nothing remarkable had happened so far. We had a fire drill during second period, but that was it.

As fourth period was coming to an end, my class talked with each other, played on our phones, oblivious to anything else, really. Another fire drill interrupted our conversation.

We all exchanged looks but didn't think much else of it. It was odd to have multiple fire drills in the same day, but we just went with it. As I walked outside my classroom, I gazed at the

Freshman Building. I was right next to it. It was in this moment I heard the first shots.

Of course I didn't know they were shots at the time. I figured a balloon popped, a textbook dropped, a door slammed, it could have been anything. I didn't give it another thought.

Every classroom in the school has a specific route during a fire drill. My classroom and the ones around it all needed to go to the senior lot and stand outside of the Freshman Building.

As I made my way to the staircase that leads down to the Freshman Building, an administrator urged me to go back up. "Go! Go! Get the hell back!" he said. I was utterly confused. Why is this man screaming at me about a fire drill? Even if it was a real fire, it was most likely in the Culinary Room, hopefully contained, and I wasn't in any danger.

So I went to another staircase, the one that leads to the red gates of the school. As I closed in on the steps, yet another administrator told me to go back the way I came. "Whatever, I know what I'm doing. I'm going to the senior lot," I thought.

As I made my way back to the first staircase I went to, I felt a sensation that can only be described as eerie. I walked down the steps and almost laid eyes on the base of the Freshman Building.

Then I heard it.

It is said that the human brain only processes about 17 to 25 percent of what is picked up through the ears. I can guarantee you I processed every shrilling decibel of that moment.

There are certain sounds you cannot mistake.

I sprinted back up the stairs and locked eyes on my classroom. As I reached for the door handle and attempted to open it, the door wouldn't budge. I'm really not sure how to describe my feeling in that moment. A sense of despair yet understanding is how I could phrase it.

It is protocol for all teachers to lock their doors during a Code Red. I just never thought I'd be on the receiving end.

More shots went off. I didn't know if they were real or if my mind was just manifesting more sounds to frighten me further.

I found myself and a handful of students locked outside of all the classrooms.

Not a single one welcomed us.

We ended up making our way to an outside hallway intersection. Someone told us to stay there. I'm not sure if he was an administrator, substitute, student, or what. It didn't matter. This was the safest place we could be in the moment.

I could still see the side of the Freshman Building from where we stood.

I guess you could say it was somewhat of an advantage. Being able to see from three directions brought a sense of comfort. It told us that we had other options if we were approached by the shooter from one of the hallways.

We waited. It was only around five minutes, but it felt like hours.

It is hard to text your family that there is an active shooter on campus. I know that my father didn't necessarily believe me. "Are you serious?" he asked.

I called my mom, kept her updated, but I didn't really know what to say. I remember her telling me that they brought a big guy into an ambulance. I can only surmise she was referring to Coach Feis, but I'm willing to bet he was unrecognizable.

From the corner of my eye, I saw a door open, and in the span of five seconds, everyone piled into the room.

I'm not big on exercise, but in that moment, everyone was on the track team.

We huddled in a corner and stayed out of sight from the window.

I didn't know who the teacher was; after all, there are many teachers in the school, and they don't get to teach every student. I remember her saying something along the lines of "I want you to know that if anyone comes through that door, they will have to go through me."

I would later find out that her name is Mrs. Trizzino.

I'm an avid video game player, but nothing I've ever played compares to the raw intensity of the SWAT team that entered the classroom around two hours later.

SWAT stands for Special Weapons and Tactics. It was very interesting to come to the realization that a place of education had become one of blood and death.

We marched out in a single-file line and made it to the intersection, where my mom was waiting.

I had told her I wanted to go get burgers with her that day, so she had been waiting on the intersection for the entire duration of the shooting.

I worried for her too, because ultimately, a stray bullet is a stray bullet.

I don't really remember much else from that day. I don't even remember falling asleep. Even now time seems . . . distorted. There is no routine. No daily ritual. Nothing to revolve my days around.

I still haven't cried yet.

I wonder what that means.

SECOND FIRE DRILL
by Sabrina Yuen-Orozco

Ring
(Fire alarm starts)
(Speaking)
"Ugh, another fire alarm? What did culinary do now?"
(Inside my head)
"Do we really need to go? It's so close to school
    ending. Can't I just leave?"
"It's Valentine's Day, of all days. They've decided to
    cause a fire today?"
Boom
(Inside my head)
"Is that a backpack dropping?"
"Why would someone drop their backpack from the
    second floor during a fire drill?"
"Another backpack?"
"There's no way three people have dropped three
    backpacks from the second floor."
"What is that noise, then?"

"Why is everyone running towards me?"
(Speaking)
"STOP!"
"What are you doing?"
"Stop pushing me."
"Ouch! Stop! Why are you kicking me to the floor?"
"Someone please help me."

The World Is Moving On
by Alexis Gendron

The world is moving on & I have not. I am glued to the ground. I am trapped in the building—not physically, but spiritually. That day still plays in my head like a movie on repeat. Each time it plays, some terrible new detail is remembered.

I'm lost and feel as though I will never find my way out of this nightmare. I constantly dream about it . . . when I do actually get some sleep. I'm in the building again, but this time everyone is gone and it's just me . . . the doors all locked . . . blood everywhere. I can hear screaming, but can't find anyone. Then I see him standing at the end of the hall with no expression on his face. He chases me through the building and I have nowhere to hide, just like that day I hid in plain sight.

Everyone sees me and says I'm getting better and I'm doing great, but they aren't me. Just because I seem okay on the outside doesn't mean I truly am. It's as if I'm here, but not here . . . as if I am me, but not me . . . how can this be?

The world seems to be happy & I should be too, but I am not the world and I am not you . . . I'm not even me. I'm someone else now, and this new person doesn't like fireworks, knocking on doors or walls, loud popping noises, the sound of glass shattering. Nor do I like people screaming & I don't like the sounds of phones ringing.

I'm fine. I'm okay.

Immortal Dreams
by Augustus Griffith Jr.

Death is a daily, natural thing. Everyone's time runs out
Sometime, everybody's gotta go. But there's nothing scarier than
being forgotten. Don't let me be forgotten.

I hope you write about me
Never forget about me
Heard what you said about me
  I can relate

My pen's an influence

Remember all the rants that I wrote
And all the questions I posed
What comes around goes
I often have dreams of you dyin'
I'm screaming, I'm crying
They come around so often
Now I'm in the coffin

So many problems packed
Inside the words, I miss you
Celebrating my life but people don't party with tissues
If I could inspire just one person
Fuel the fire
With just one verse then
I'll still live on
Remember me when I'm gone
Write about me.

HOW A DOG'S LOVE CHANGED MY LIFE
by Grace Briden

After everything that happened, I never wanted to go back to school ever again. Even though it had been days since my world changed, it was still emotionally impossible to adjust. Once I walked into school, everything I saw triggered me. I began to have flashbacks everywhere I went. In the hallway, in the bathroom, in class, or really anywhere, I would be forced into remembering everything that happened that day. I really couldn't focus because all I could think of was my friends and classmates who had been murdered and that they would never be able to see their friends or families ever again. They never even got to say goodbye. I felt selfish when I was happy about my close friends and teachers being alive. I was overcome with sadness when I went into my JROTC and missed seeing two of my classmates and realized that they would never come to class again. I was angry about choosing this high school as the first high school I went to in the US. All of these emotions were flooding my body and mind at the same time. On top of that, I had friends and family and even enemies from other countries and states asking if I was okay and asking me to tell them what happened. Everyone wanted to know my story, and if I shared it,

I would have to experience the pain of it all over again. I had never gone through something like this, and I didn't know what to do with my emotions or feelings at all. There is no protocol on how to get through this and try to accept what has happened. Healing after the shooting was a very hard thing to do.

Honestly, I never thought I would be able to get over what happened, but that was when I met the therapy dogs. At first, I didn't believe the dogs could help with what I was feeling, but they actually did. Their love and happiness just made my life better! Petting them calmed me down, and cuddling up with them was so sweet, I couldn't help but smile! It was the first time I felt happy since the shooting. I don't know what I would have done or where I would be without them. Daisy, Emma, Karma, Grace, Jett, and Addie were the therapy dogs who were always there for me. Their puppy love made me so happy and I truly felt so loved! Their handlers were so sweet and dedicated to helping me with whatever I needed! All of those amazing therapy dogs inspired me to make my own dog a therapy dog. When I saw how much these dogs helped me heal, I realized that my dog could do the same. It was amazing to see how my dog, Duncan, could make people happy by just being himself. It helped me deal with my grief and sadness by seeing Duncan help people who truly needed it. These therapy dogs led me to my calling to help people who need some loving from dogs just like I needed after the shooting.

Photo by Marni Bellavia

Duncan and I are trained
and ready to help others.

Photo by Lori Bale

One Month and Ten Days
by Kaitlyn Puller

On February 14, 2018,
I was running with my friend
in order to catch up with others.
We were running with questions in our minds
and a sense of innocence that I'd never get back.

On March 24, 2018,
I was running with my friend
in order to catch up with others.
We were running with signs held up high
and a sense of pride that I'd never felt before.

At 3:00 on February 14,
I was holding my phone in my left hand
and my friend's hand in my right.
She was crying.
She said to me, with a look of fear in her eyes,
"I can't believe this is happening."

At 12:00 on March 24,
I was holding part of a sign in my left hand
and my friend's hand in my right.
She was crying.
She said to me, with a look of hope in her eyes,
"I can't believe this is happening."

Photo by Natasha Martinez

Nothing Bad Ever Happens in Parkland
TESTIMONY BEFORE CONGRESS

(This is the original speech Stacey Lippel brought to Congress.)
March 20, 2018
by Stacey Lippel, language arts instructor at MSD

On February 14, I spent the day at school like any other day in room 1255 on the third floor of the 1200 building, also known as the Freshman Building, at Marjory Stoneman Douglas High School. It was Valentine's Day and the kids were happy and excited as they walked through the halls with their oversized stuffed animals, oversized balloons, and oversized energy level. It was fourth period and I had just taught my creative writing class how to write the perfect love letter. They were animated and silly. Meadow Pollack wrote a letter to her longtime boyfriend. She told me they were together for four years. Joaquin Oliver resisted this assignment because he already got his girlfriend plenty of things, but I told him a handwritten note would go very far. He proceeded to write love notes on cutout hearts and taped them to his shirt. My students told me that he did write an actual love letter but put it in his backpack.

Then everything changed.

At about 2:20, we heard a popping sound that sounded like a computer cart fell over. The class was loud so the sound was muted. Approximately two minutes later, the fire alarm sounded. It was unusual because we had already had a drill that morning, but I knew that the culinary classes were cooking with oil, so evacuating was nothing I would have even hesitated doing. So many scenarios popped into my head at that moment . . . fire in culinary, maybe that sound was firecrackers and there was actually a fire. I never, ever thought that this was a result of gunshots because the context wouldn't have made any sense.

We live in Parkland.

Nothing bad ever happens in Parkland.

I shouted above the alarm to my students that I would be taking attendance at our usual spot, grabbed my emergency folder and phone, then waited for the last student to exit before I closed and locked my door behind me. I walked about two feet from my door when I heard the gunshots down in the stairwell. The stairwell is about twenty feet away from my classroom. All of the students who were in the stairwell started screaming and running back the other way (toward me and the other classrooms). I quickly turned around, unlocked my door, and then very quickly ensured that the lock was back in a locked position so that when I shut the door the lock would already be locked on the outside. (I don't know how else to describe this action, but it's very important because it truly saved my life and the lives of my students.) Shots were firing and students were pouring into my class: kids who were mine, kids who I had never seen before. I held my door open and pulled kids in as I watched the scene unfold before my eyes. I saw the shooter emerge from the stairwell and stand very firmly at the front of the hall about twenty feet from me. He was constantly shooting as he sprayed his rifle back and forth. I don't know how he didn't hit more kids with all of the bullets flying in the hallway.

It was foggy with smoke, but I kept my eye on the shooter.

His head and face were covered. I thought it was a helmet and a gas mask. He also had on what I thought was a bullet-proof vest, but I later found out that it was a vest that held ammunition. I originally described him as having on "full metal garb" because that was my perception at the time. All I know is that he looked like a MAN with a very menacing weapon in his hand. I remember thinking, "Is this real? What is going on here? Why is this man shooting at us?" But I never broke from my task at hand: to get as many kids into my room as possible and get that door shut. I was in autopilot mode. I don't remember screaming. I definitely wasn't crying. I just knew that saving my students and myself was very important. I don't know when I decided now was the time to close my door, but I did. I shouted at Mr. Scott Beigel to close his door because his classroom was right next to mine and he was ushering students into his room just as I was. I grabbed the door handle with both hands (my left arm crossing my body) because I wanted to make sure I pulled it tight. It was then that I was grazed by a bullet. I remember feeling a little sting but soon forgot it. As I was shutting my door, two of my students wanted to get in as they were still in the hall. Understand that even though there were still kids running in the hall, I had to make a decision to shut my door or risk getting shot and putting the students in my room in danger. I don't remember reopening the door. They told me I did. I opened it a crack, Mr. Beigel shoved them in, then I pulled my door closed and hung on to the handle for a few more seconds to ensure it was really, really closed (another action I don't remember, but my students told me I did this).

I jumped over to the blind spot in my room where I trained my students to go when we had a Code Red. I threw myself on top of my students and held on to as many as I could sink my nails into. Seconds later I heard a barrage of shots in Mr. Beigel's room, then immediately after that, the shooter fired about four or five times right into my classroom through the glass panel in the door. I remember stretching my neck to see if he was going to reach in and grab the door handle through the broken glass. I don't know why he didn't. He could have easily entered the classroom and shot us all, but he didn't. He continued to fire shots down the hallway. I kept looking at the clock and thinking, "This is definitely not a drill. School should be over soon." These were strange and random thoughts we all had because even though we were living this nightmare, it just seemed impossible that this was happening.

This is Parkland.

Nothing bad ever happens in Parkland.

I kept staring at the shattered glass on the floor, as well as the bullet casings. I counted at least four or five. We all heard a boy screaming in the hallway, "HELP! OPEN THE DOOR! HELP! LET ME IN!" But we couldn't open the door. The shooter could still be on the floor. If I opened the door, I would put us all at risk. So we cringed every time we heard the screaming.

Students were texting their loved ones. I texted my coworker who was on the other side of the school that there was a shooter in my building. My son was in her class. My daughter was in a classroom close to the other side of the school as well. I knew they were safe. I don't remember texting my husband. I don't remember answering texts from concerned family and friends. I deleted all of my texts that night because it made me sick to my stomach to look back at them. I spent the next hour making eye contact with my students, holding on to them, and mouthing that everything was going to be okay.

When the SWAT team arrived, I still didn't get up to open the door. What if it's the shooter? They barged in, pointed their guns at us, and ordered us to put our hands up in the air just in case the shooter was among us. One of the men pointed at me and asked, "Teacher?" I said yes, and he asked me to make sure my students didn't look down as we left the classroom. I stood up and immediately saw the body of Scott Beigel on the ground. I couldn't process that he was dead until a student looked at him and screamed. I went into teacher mode and ordered her to look up. We stepped out of the classroom and saw carnage everywhere. There were bullet casings, smoke, shattered glass, blood, and bodies throughout the hallway.

It was a war zone.

I still couldn't process what I was seeing.

We live in Parkland.

Nothing bad ever happens in Parkland.

Students screamed and cried as they looked down and saw their classmates dead on the ground. I grabbed them and pushed them down the stairs and finally out of the building. My two beautiful students, Meadow and Joaquin, who were finishing up their senior year on a high note, were brutally murdered. My heart breaks for their families and aches for the loss I feel. I knew them both since they were sophomores.

I do not know how I wasn't killed. I should have been killed. I am thankful that I reacted the way I did because my students needed me to be there for them, but they are all scarred. Students aren't coming to school because they don't feel safe. It is so difficult to heal because now, in the aftermath, we are learning about so many warning signs . . . so many red flags. I am scared, sad, and angry at the same time. I lost my classroom, my security, and my confidence in people to do their jobs, but I stand strong for my family and my students while I try to cope the best way I can.

Why I Walk Out
by Samantha Deitsch

I walk out for those who can't.

I walk out to stand up for what I believe in.

I walk out to exercise my freedom.

I walk out to make a difference.

I walk out for the future of our country.

I walk out so more people have futures that aren't demolished by gun violence.

I walk out for Alyssa.

I walk out for Mr. Beigel.

I walk out for Martin.

I walk out for Nick.

I walk out for Coach Feis.

I walk out for Jaime.

I walk out for Coach Hixon.

I walk out for Luke.

I walk out for Cara.

I walk out for Gina.

I walk out for Guac.

I walk out for Alaina.

I walk out for Meadow.

I walk out for Helena.

I walk out for Alex.

I walk out for Carmen.

I walk out for Peter.

I walk out for a better tomorrow.

Happy Birthday
By Chloe Rogers

Since you've been gone, time has
      flown by.
All of our memories stay in my heart.
Today you turn 15, and you're not
   here to celebrate.
Over these past few months, my
   life has gone downhill,
I put flowers on your grave
and tears rolled down my cheek.
I wish you were here to tell me
      It's okay
I wish we could go to the beach,
make eachother laugh, kick a
soccerball one more time.
   Happy birthday to you, Alyssa.
Without you, life is just so blue.

Photo by Rain Valladares

Dear Senator Marco Rubio

My name is Leni Steinhardt, and I am currently a tenth grader at Marjory Stoneman Douglas High School in Parkland, Florida. On February 14, I ran for my life in fear that I would lose it. I called my parents one last time to tell them I loved them, just in case I never got to again. I heard gunshots go off and chaos around me. Why does this sound like a war zone? THIS IS A SCHOOL I'M TALKING ABOUT. More importantly, *my school* that I am talking about.

Allow me to reintroduce myself: my name is Leni Steinhardt, and I am a survivor of a school shooting. That is a sentence no sixteen-year-old should have to write. My innocence was stripped away from me as I lost my classmates and faculty to gun violence. I can still see the chaos in the hallways when I close my eyes. I am traumatized. For two hours, I hid in fear that I would die, until a SWAT team rescued me. For two hours, a high schooler should be playing video games, doing homework, or learning a math lesson. For two hours, a student should not be cramped up in the corner of a dark classroom hiding while their classmates are being murdered. I want to scream at the top of my lungs, "Why?" Why did my brother have to lose one of his close friends? Why did I have to run for my life in fear that I would be shot?

Why did I have to call my parents and say "I love you" one last time in case I never got to again? Why did this have to be my school? Why is my school a crime scene now? Why did this happen? All of these thoughts now consume my mind day and night.

I am mentally exhausted and drained. However, I can no longer cry. I can no longer think of the what-ifs. I look around at my amazing community coming together at a time like this, asking the government to evoke policy and change. Here is my question to you: What are you and the rest of the government doing to prevent this from happening again? What are you doing to heal the pain that I am feeling? What are you going to do next? Please, I beg of you, never let this happen again.

Sincerely,

Leni Steinhardt

Parkland, FL
Marjory Stoneman Douglas Class of 2020

Photo by Natasha Martinez

Attempts at Acceptance
by Samantha Bonnin

This has been every whirlwind set in motion
My neurons have gone through a blender
And I am here, so far away from any logical
    explanation
But here I am, alive
Pushing through the sadness, pulling myself out of
    the breakdowns
Crossing so many lines and watching tension rise
    and give
As if fate itself needs to take deep breaths

But it is life
A life I had never imagined, one that went just
    beyond the prophet's lens
Because no one could ever foresee Parkland's
    perfectly manicured lawns
Being stained with blood
No one would ever predict the lives of the
    sheltered
Being so radically changed by unparalleled pain and
    tragedy
Yet, when Nikolas Cruz made his way past the doors
    of the freshmen building
Cruel irony began crashing through the crevices of
    fate like a flood

And then in under seven unspeakable minutes,
    life was cut short for seventeen Eagles
And irreparably frayed for countless others

So yes, this is life
A life in which mass shooting has become synonymous
    with MSD
A life in which I still cannot wrap my mind around the
    fact that I will never see Carmen again
A life of more ups and downs than an unsteady
    rollercoaster,
But it is a life of hope
Or at least what I have been desperately trying to
    perceive as hope
Because through all the pain, the sleepy eyes of the
    nation have awoken to creeping rays of change
And 800,000 of us marched on Washington
Demanding that the tragedy of Parkland is never
    repeated
That no one ever again has to watch their city turn
    into a national sensation
With the words "massacre" printed on every headline
Because as my world has been under the magnifying
    glass
And my classmates have become celebrities
My community works toward making sure this
    insufferable pain was not in vain
That the death of seventeen people was not in vain

And I keep fighting
I keep going
There is no looking back

Political Puppets
BY ANNA KASPERSKI

Would you believe me if I told you Pinocchio is alive?
He's more than just a little wooden toy.
His nose gets bigger each time he lies
And cannot hide it, what a poor boy.

You've read of him in fairy tales
In a land far, far away.
What if I were to tell you in detail
The truth behind his painted display?

He makes promises to us, The People.
He claims he always keeps his word.
The things he says leave us all gleeful
But the whispers behind the closed doors go unheard.

He listens to the Corrupted
Because of the money they bring.
After all he is just a puppet
That only works if someone plays with his strings.

Pinocchio does not live as far as you think.
He's probably lying to someone right about now.
Never can think for himself and always lip syncs
Information the Corrupted always put down.

Soon we will see the growing nose
And recognize his filthy lies.
We will all come together to try to expose
And tear apart this puppet's disguise.

We have had enough of this fraud
Preaching things only if he gets bribed.
We're completely done with his painted facade
Not listening to us after so many have died.

Pinocchio is your fellow political figures,
Their strings being played by "patriotic people."
They clog their ears with money to muffle the trigger
And praise our flag as we drape it over our fallen eagles.

This is not the Pinocchio that I grew up on.
This world we live in is not a children's story.
I will not be manipulated like a pawn
And watch these puppets bask in their ugly glory.

Let's keep Pinocchio in the storybooks where
    he belongs
And fight these crooks with no apologies.
Together we will all stand strong
And fix this country's broken democracy.

don't shoot: please
by Samantha Deitsch

you say you love your guns
well i love my friends
a life is irreplaceable
a life has value
more value than a gun
it's shocking how some people disagree
at the end of a day you chose a gun over me

don't shoot
please don't shoot
don't shoot in my school
don't shoot in my theatre
don't shoot at the church
don't shoot up the streets
please keep the guns in the range or for
    hunting and safety

With great power comes great responsibility
with fire power comes great responsibility
please don't shoot
it's not too late to help the youth feel safe
the innocence is there if you let kids be kids
let teachers teach and not face a gun

don't shoot
please don't shoot
please don't shoot me
please don't shoot my friends
please don't shoot my family
i wish you wouldn't shoot the
    innocent, the neighbors, the
        teachers, the children, the innocent.
please stop shooting the innocent
don't shoot

Case Number 18001958CF10A
by Caitlynn Tibbetts

I don't say your name.
You don't exist.
You don't exist.
You don't exist.

I go deaf when you're on the tip of someone else's
    tongue.
The value of those words drain me as if oxygen is
    being depleted from my lungs.
The memory of you is still as sharp and crisp as
    paper—the plastic hasn't even been ripped off yet.

Has it been three months?
It feels like three years.
It feels like three seconds.

I go blind when your face is on a screen.
I prefer simply darkness now, where at least I can
    find comfort in the familiarity.
There are no snaps, no twists, no surprises with
    darkness.
It is constant.

You are just another stranger, just another
    combination of shamelessness and evil.
Maybe I have seen you before.
You look different.

Is that a new mask?

I go mute when you are brought up in a
    conversation.
My thoughts jumble like puzzle pieces.
Except nothing fits.
I can never put two and two together.
I wish I didn't know you.
I wish no one knew you.
I wish there remained the same amount of
    people in my first period.
My wishes have been proven fruitless.

Are you happy?
People know you.
Thousands do.

I don't say your name.
You don't exist.
You don't exist.
You don't exist.

A Zoo Animal
by Rebecca Schneid

I feel like a zoo animal,
always on display for the world to see.
Locked in a cage where people can judge me,
but I can't even see myself.

I don't even know myself.

Sometimes I think that I am fine,
that I've lost some of that sheer pain and wrath;
that I'm on a path
towards healing and success,
towards not moving on really, but growing
from the distress
and the stress of the press
and the emotions I repress
so I can solely focus on this country's lack of progress.

I think that I'm fine
until I find myself dreaming about the screams I heard
    all that time ago.
The confusion.
The fear.
The barrel of a gun in the face of those who I hold
    dear,
bullets in the heads of my peers.

I dream that it was me.
That I died and not my friends.
Most days I wish that's how it did end—
with me gone and them here ready to ascend,
to make this world better like they should've been able to.

I won't sit here and pretend
like I can go back and change it.
I can't.
None of us can.

If I could, I would in a split second.
We can take this hand that G-d has granted us and use
    it to take a stand
against a government that refuses to listen to our
    demands,
refuses to recognize the enormity of this movement
    that *we* began.

We take a stand against those who hear us screaming
    but refuse to listen,
who claim to be so wholesome and Christian.
They turn their backs on the 96 people who die from
    gun violence
every day like it's a tradition.
Is this the country our founding fathers envisioned?

One where money and power and ambition
blind our leaders to this American condition
of getting shot wherever we go.
While some may have bullets,
our voices must be our ammunition.
Those we have lost, and the pain that has arisen
must be the ignition

to a flame that will cross this great nation
and lead to a transition.

That is our mission.
A transition to a world where school isn't a prison,
where our deaths aren't already written
at the hands of a gun in
a concert
or a club
or a place of worship.

For the lack of a better term,
the bullet *must* be bitten.

I know it must be hard to give up
your donations and your power,
the support of an organization that keeps you
blind in your ivory tower.
Down here we see clearly.
While you cower up there
(and I say this sincerely)

WE ARE DYING.

And not just us from MSD,
those from Baltimore, Chicago, and Washington, DC

You turn your backs on them too.
You have for far too long.

Minorities and the poor,
living in neighborhoods where every day gun violence
    is endured.
Where every day they scream for change but are
    ignored

because of their income, or their race,
or because they are "too young and immature."

We have a *birthright*
to life, liberty, and the pursuit of happiness.
A piece of which is lost with every single gunfight.

Sometimes I imagine
where I would be
if this didn't happen.
If we didn't have to take our pain
and turn it into action.
If so many other parts of my life
didn't fall apart as a reaction
to this wildfire of hate.
Not an overreaction,
a nuclear reaction,
a complex fraction,
breaking this fragile happiness that I had built,
ruining my satisfaction.

With my life.

With me.

Sometimes I think that I am fine
because I smile and I laugh,
but underneath I cry and I kick and I grit my teeth.
I did not just lose 17 fellow Eagles on February
    fourteenth.
I lost a piece of myself

I lost who I was.
I lost most of my friends.
I lost my love.

I lost my ability to breathe without needing strength
     from up above
to do it.

I lost my innocence.
I lost my ability to believe
there is goodness in all those who show wickedness,
because there is not.

Sometimes I am so full of emotions and feelings
it's like I'm bleeding, and they are oozing out.
I am healing, but also reeling with these thoughts
that keep my head wheeling with this tragedy's
     possible meaning.

Then I am numb,
and I feel none.

I am empty; I am worn.
And I am so, so sad
and so, so done.

Done with the way this country is run,
because how can you tell *me*
that a gun
is not the reason for this pain within
me and everyone.

Some people tell us to wait:
"We must be patient."
"We cannot exploit the deaths of our classmates."
Well, that *frustrates* me.

People die every day.
You remain blind and think that this country can
    be great
without legislation that attempts to eliminate the hate.

Because the revolution is not waiting,
the revolution is not coming.
The revolution is *now*, it is *angry,* it is *hungry,*
and it is becoming a force to be reckoned with.

I realize that I don't just feel like a zoo animal.
I *am* a zoo animal.
I have been a zoo animal.
These bars have been around me
for so long that I am conditioned to think it is normal.
It is not.

So, while we may not be immortal,
this passion, this fervor,
this persistence for a resistance is.

We will not rest until these bars are broken.
Until we are zoo animals no more
but instead free of the shackles we once bore.

Dear Mr. President
by Alyson Sheehy

My friends have died, they are gone from our lives,
Yet you sit there, twiddling your thumbs.
My friends have died, the life gone from their eyes,
Yet you sit there, talking anything but guns.

My friends have died, and we've cried and cried,
Yet you sit there, blaming the mentally ill.
My friends have died, our voices pushed aside,
Yet you sit there, you sit there still.

My friends have died, and our tears aren't dried,
Yet you sit there, watching us plead.
My friends have died, an issue nationwide,
You sit there still, so how 'bout you lead?

As a community forever unified,
I ask you, sir, how did this happen to us?
I invite you to learn, to hear the story from inside,
Cause if not now, when will the right time be to discuss?

Photo by Natasha Martinez

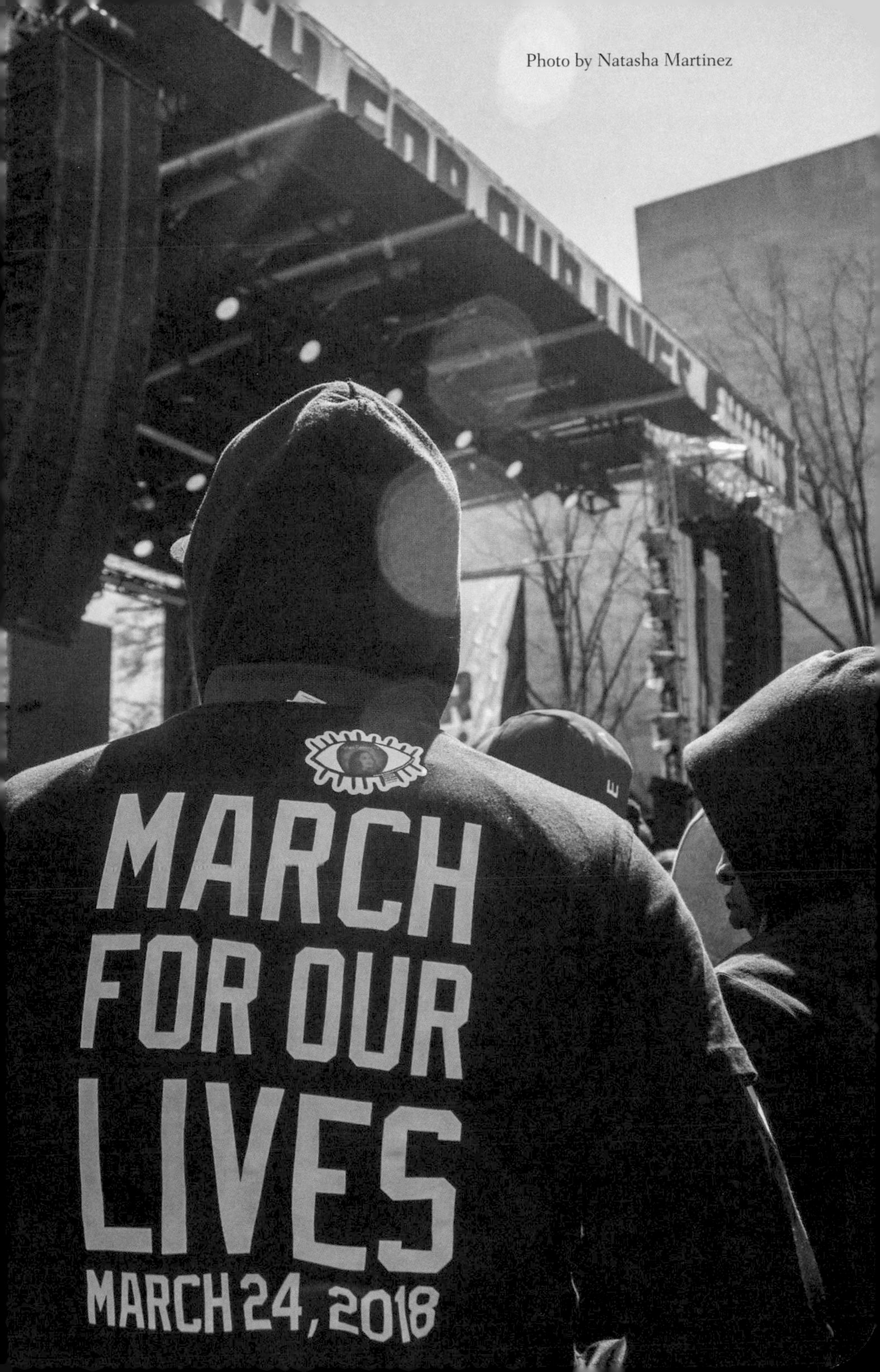

The Metaphors and Realities of Death
by Samantha Bonnin

Death used to be a metaphor
It was a stylistic thing
It was dramatic and captivating
And a dash was thrown into each
Lament of heartbreak or commiseration of stress
It was everywhere in words
But it was nonchalant
A devil-may-care phrase
And it was as if being at the edge of it
Was as routine as a walk in the park
But now it has lost its nonchalance
It's so real it's tangible
And it hides in the back of all my nightmares
It's no longer dramatic and long and drawn out
It's abrupt and spontaneous
It's unexpected
And it's permanent
It's no longer stylistic
It's just an inevitable cruelty of life
that could happen at any moment

Photo by Sam Grizelj

Photo by Rain Valladares

Dreamer
by Augustus Griffith Jr.

Somebody said you walked for me
You fought, you bled,
Got shot for me,
Preached enough to part a sea
You fought for me, you fought for we
You did it all nonviolently
And that means the world to me.
You fought for us, time and again,
Against the artisans of sin
If we had words like yours around,
We wouldn't feel so broken down
If you came back, I'm not sure how
It'd mean the world to me
Somebody said, since King is dead,
The world's turned cold.
That's all I know.
Who's gonna teach us how to love?
Who's gonna show us when to cry?
They can say this place is just,
The only voice we hear just died
I wish Gandhi were alive, and that we had peace of mind
I want to be a lover, but I gotta be a fighter
I'll burn for another, just as fuel for the fire
I could've sworn this world was free
I swear to God this world hates me
I swear to God,
My black don't crack, but everyone wants a piece of mine

Behind "Protected" Doors
Valentine's Day—Freshman Building of Stoneman Douglas High School
BY MADALYN SNYDER

Valentine's Day has always been my favorite holiday. I adore the smell of blooming flowers, and the cheap cliché gifts that are generally purchased last minute. Enormous plush animals being dragged down hallways and courtyards, and chocolate candy wrappers coating the floor, overfilling trash cans. The occasional raging girlfriend disappointed in her boyfriend while nearby observers are entertained by the ridiculous behavior of a self-absorbed, spoiled girl; feeling sympathy and empathy for him for having no experience with pleasing the female gender. Nevertheless, I love surrounding myself with the Valentine's Day moments between couples. Although some people are left without a partner, or with a "difficult to please" partner, there is always love to go around to anyone who wants it. Valentine's Day is the celebration of love for one another, and a beautiful day for people to get together.

On Valentine's Day I arrived at Stoneman Douglas and began looking enviously over at those enjoying the morning with their Valentine's Day sweethearts: holding their massive teddy bears, bouquets of roses with saccharine baby's breath, and basking in the immense feelings of warmth that I was quietly missing. I stared at them, wanting to have all the same things they did, as anyone would. My own valentine had texted and called me the night before, saying he wouldn't be in school with me that day because of an anxiety attack.

In first period math class, I was relieved to see my friends Duffy, Jacob, and Guac. Duffy made me a card with a heart saying "From Your Valentine" when he overheard me telling Jacob that my valentine was at home. Duffy is always such a sweetheart. He reminds me of my older sister Fallon, and I admire him unconditionally.

When we were going over the homework in class, my teacher, Mr. Gard, asked Guac to answer one of the questions. Unfortunately, Guac had copied my homework earlier that morning and made a mistake rewriting the problem. After being marked incorrect, he sarcastically yelled at me, saying, "Well, maybe if your 4s didn't look like 9s!" I chuckled under my breath.

Later that day during second period, we had a fire drill. Drills were not an unusual occurrence, and they were carefully planned in order to catch students off guard, though rumors always seemed to escape the careless mouths of the staff without consequence. Because of this, we were never surprised when the alarm went off.

From there I was released to lunch, where I ran into Helena, whom I had met through mutual friends. She was one of the sweetest girls I had the opportunity to meet since I began at Stoneman Douglas. From what I had seen of her, she was always compassionate to everyone, and I was lucky enough to have had the chance to spend time with her and her friends outside of school. I asked her to sit at our lunch table, but she had already made plans to sit with another group of friends that day. Being the sweetheart that she was, she said hello to many people before walking across the courtyard to enjoy her lunch with friends.

Toward the end of the day, during fourth block, I began to walk to Mrs. Lippel's class, which was my creative writing period. I thought about calling my father to sign me out early to spare myself from having to write a half-assed assignment that I'd receive a 100 percent on, regardless of depth or color. But for some unexplainable reason, I felt a compelling need to go to class that day, and I regrettably decided to remain in school, despite my negative opinion of the course.

I didn't spend a lot of time writing during the period because the class was too unfulfilling. I couldn't wait for it to be over and ached to jump out of my skin. Those ninety minutes sitting in that uncomfortable orange plastic seat entirely covered in graffiti with mutilated gum stuck underneath felt like a total waste of time. But since I'd gotten so many zeroes for all the assignments I'd never handed in, I figured I might as well try to save myself from failing the course and do some makeup work.

Regardless of how much I abhor my creative writing class, my admiration for Mrs. Lippel continued to grow. If she hadn't been there for me throughout the year, I might not have succeeded. Not because I couldn't handle the course, but because of the unbearable boredom I would have had to endure on my own without her. Not only is she like a second mother to me and to everyone else in the class, but she made me feel unique even when I felt lost. She always made herself available to those who were in need of advice, or was simply someone to confide in. And she always found delight in reading my pieces, even when I thought they were utterly disappointing.

As I entered Room 1225, I thought I'd hand in some over-due assignments to prove to Mrs. Lippel that I was, at the very least, trying. Not because of my grade but because I felt the need to show her that I wasn't the irresponsible screwup I was making myself out to be. I was able to sit down and finish my latest assignment—writing a love letter or a love-to-hate let-ter. My friend Guac shared this class with me, and we began talking about how we were going to spend Valentine's Day. He had planned on enjoying the rest of his day with his girlfriend, Tori, hand in hand. I felt undeniably jealous of him, wishing that I was able to do the same with my valentine. Putting my emotions aside, I couldn't help but smile widely for him. A few weeks earlier, I'd asked Guac when he and Tori had first met. He paused and said, "We met in another lifetime, and we meet in every single lifetime."

As we continued talking, we both began cutting heart-shaped construction paper to give to our valentines. I could tell that it brought him just as much excitement to write cute sayings on each heart as it did me. He began to tape his heart to his clothing as I argued that the tape wouldn't keep the paper heart from falling off. He insisted that he'd rather tape it than puncture his peachy-pink shirt with staples. I laughed at him and impetuously stapled my cutout heart to my thin black jacket.

Nearly fifteen minutes before the bell was to ring, I heard pandemonium outside our classroom. I slowly turned my head from the doorway to look at my teacher with intense consuming fear in my chest. I frantically asked, "What was that?" She immediately got up to make sure the door was locked. On occasion the door was left cracked open in case a student was late to class. As she was checking the door, the abrupt and rapid sound became clearer.

My classmates began making jokes, saying it sounded like a gun. Guac jokingly ran and hid in the closet by the door. After a moment, the noise from the class faded into what I could only describe as a sort of black silence. The kind of silence that makes you question your present reality; the kind that turns your skin cold at the thought of the ominous possibilities surrounding your heart with fear. The silence was shattered when the fire alarm went off for the second time that day. My heart sank, because there was no reasonable explanation for why a fire drill would have started this close to the end of the day.

Immediately, all of my classmates began panicking and rushing to evacuate the room. As students filed out in frightened disorder, I waited for my teacher just outside the class door. When everyone had left the room, she followed with a fire drill folder held tightly in her arms. I attempted to persuade her to stay inside, saying, "This is too much of a coincidence. I don't think we should leave." As another friend of mine walked out of the classroom, he joked obnoxiously, "That's exactly what a shooter would do! Pull the alarm so that everyone would come out of the classrooms so he could shoot us!" He then disappeared among the many students trying to exit the building, and I have not seen him since.

As Mrs. Lippel hesitantly locked the door behind us, I could tell she was scared. I was scared too, but we had to follow the fire drill regulations, which required us to evacuate.

While I waited for my teacher to accompany me out of the Freshman Building, I stood with my back to the stairs. I heard students screaming, and as I turned around they were running away from the staircase. The crowd of alarmed students frantically ran in obvious desperation to save themselves from whatever awaited them on the other end of the staircase. Suddenly I heard a voice cry out from within the crowd, "Code Red! Get back inside!" With too many people blocking the hall to run, students began stumbling over each other to get far away from the staircase as fast as possible. At this point I was unsure of what was going on. I knew it couldn't be good.

Seconds later, three shots were fired in my direction. I was sent into shock, feeling as if each bullet had pierced my body. My ears rang from the shots striking the wall, and I was paralyzed with fear as the dust covered my clothing. My face paled and my vision began to darken around the edges. My body felt completely disabled as I observed desperate students running for their lives in my direction, shoving and pushing me in a panicked frenzy. My eyes saw the desolation before me, and in that moment, fear overwhelmed all other emotions.

Confusion eclipsed my understanding of what was happening, though nothing could divert my eyes from what could very well be my impending fate. I knew it would be over soon; I had a sort of acceptance of what was to come. I was fearful, but I wasn't scared of dying. It's a different sort of feeling when it's not death itself that you fear, but the dread of the coming unknown beyond death.

The gunman began to approach me, and I could feel my heart racing. He was approximately six feet away from me when Mrs. Lippel noticed my inability to move and acted. She immediately snatched my arm, jerking me into the classroom as the gunman fired a shot in my direction. Mrs. Lippel moved me out of the way in the nick of time and, in doing so, was shot in the arm while rescuing me from death.

She remained in the doorway in order to guide more students to safety. Relief flooded my body, and for that brief moment, I felt safe. Though it soon seemed like I had razor blades in my lungs and I was unable to breathe, bringing me back to reality. Anger immediately overpowered my impotence. It was almost as if I had been hypnotized and put in a trance until Mrs. Lippel pulled me back from my half-conscious and nonresponsive state. I can't help but wonder what I might have done without her rescuing arms. Would I have remained quietly still and passively accepted my demise, or might I have run to protect others from his fatal attack? I was unable to make out his features, due to the chaos of the crowd before me blocking my line of sight. Had I remained in the hall a moment longer, I would have borne witness to the face that was responsible for all this violence and tragedy.

Instead, I ran away from the doorway and the shooter and sought the safety of a closet in the back of the classroom, which happened to be in direct sight of the window in the door. I opened the closet door, desperate for shelter, but it was filled with shelves. Realizing that it was too late to run elsewhere, I immediately climbed onto the shelves, though my body blocked the door from closing completely.

The closet became my only protection against the hell out in the hall. Because the door was partly open, I was able to see through the small crack between the hinges and the door. Then I remembered to hide my feet so they couldn't be seen at the bottom of the door.

I had no alternative, and with my back to the shelves, I felt as if I was about to vomit from fear. As I was hiding, with only a flimsy door as useless protection against bullets, multiple shots continued to fire outside my classroom. I wasn't able to think. The only thing running through my confused mind was to keep quiet and continue to hide my feet from sight. Eventually I heard the door close, but I couldn't tell if Mrs. Lippel was inside the room or if something had happened to her.

While concealing myself, I saw the gunman approach my classroom through the crack. I immediately hid my face in terror inside the closet. God forbid he happened to notice the closet door shaking from my trembling body. My heart raced as I began to hyperventilate. Fortunately, the classroom door was locked and he was unable to enter our room. I was relieved, but I began to feel the immense guilt grow sharper in my chest as he turned back to the hallway and continued his rampage, brutally murdering more defenseless students. I remained silent as

Illustration by Madalyn Snyder

I was forced to listen to the horrifying screams of agony coming from the hall. It broke my heart knowing that I couldn't run to their sides to protect them. I had to remind myself that if I left the closet to help them, I would not only be endangering myself, I would be endangering all the others who had sought safety in the classroom with me.

I wasn't sure who had made it into the classroom, but I could hear the students huddled together on the other side of the room, in locations that were not visible through the window in the classroom door. As they cried and called for help on their cell phones, I quietly prayed that the gunman would not return, and that all of this chaos would be over soon. That we would be rescued from what felt like our eternal damnation. After what seemed to be hours of hiding, everything fell completely and utterly silent.

Across the room from me was a window where I was able to see fleeing students and dozens of cop cars outside. Though the sirens were wailing, and my distraught breathing became more rapid, it was this silence that made me question every-thing I had just witnessed. Is this even real? I still hoped that this might be a drill, that the faint moans of death from the hallway weren't really the dying breaths of my fellow students.

Just a month earlier, the school's staff had gone over new regulations with students for fire drills, bomb threats, tornado drills, and intruder drills. In case of an intruder drill (Code Red), we were to seek safety along the inside walls of classrooms or other enclosed areas. They also warned us that during intruder drills, a police officer would enter our school campus, firing blanks to simulate a realistic attack against the school. During this simulation, they would assign random students to participate as victims who were either shot or missing. They said this would be "the most effective scare tactic to test students and teachers" in such a drill. I used that memory to keep myself calm, and I convinced myself that this might be the case, that maybe this whole thing was just a drill, a test.

My cell phone continuously buzzed in my left back pocket, but I couldn't reach it. At the time I wasn't sure who it was, but all those messages alarmed me. If this really was a drill, why would my cell phone be notifying me with hundreds of messages and calls? How could my family have even known? I kept turning my head to look out the window at the dozens of police officers outside the building. Eventually the moans in the hall stopped, and the only screams I heard came from outside, worried parents and students who escaped the building intact. I wondered why the police officers and SWAT team who were standing around outside hadn't come into the building yet. What are they waiting for? Has he not left the building? Are we still trapped in here with him? What are they doing out there? Why won't they just come save us?

Soon after, helicopters began flying over and news vans were attempting to gain access to the area, though they were immediately forced to evacuate the premises by the police in order to keep the area clear. I was relieved by the sight of safety outside the building, but I began to dread leaving the closet as I came to the realization that no school drill would involve multiple helicopters or hire what seemed like three hundred law enforcement officers and rescue workers in order to seem "realistic." In that closet I could still pretend that this whole thing was simply simulated to scare us and that in the morning everything would be as it would any other day.

I felt like I would faint if I didn't attempt to move my body soon. I decided to risk giving away my location by quietly turning around in the closet to relieve the stress on my hips and lower back. Cautiously I waited a moment longer, staying completely still, to make sure that I hadn't given away my location. As I waited, my classmates spoke quietly, informing each other that they had heard something moving in the closet. I leaned out in order to show them that it was only me, but when I did, their faces seemed terrified that I was exposed to danger by being in front of the classroom door. I saw only a few people I didn't know. I was hoping to see my teacher, but I couldn't lean out far enough to see everyone in the classroom with me.

Now that I had shifted my position, I could reach my cell phone. Disregarding the messages, I pressed the record icon to have some sort of evidence of this dreadful moment. After setting the cell phone to record, I placed it on a stack of papers in front of me to reduce the sound of the vibrations and to maintain a clear audio recording.

I continued looking out the window to see if anyone had been coming for us, or if the shooter was being arrested outside the building. To my disappointment I wasn't able to identify what was occurring outside. I began to breathe harder as I heard a loud bang from somewhere inside the building—a bang as if someone had broken through a jammed door. I soon recognized the voices as officers of some sort. Finally, I heard the same faint voices grow clearer as they approached our classroom from the hallway. It was obvious to me that these men had come to rescue us from the hell that had once been our classroom. In order to gain access to the classroom, they had to break through the glass on the door. As they raced into the room with their guns raised to check the perimeter, tears began to fall from my eyes for the first time since the shooting began. This was the only time I felt remotely safe enough to weep.

I was overwhelmed with relief as I realized that we had made it. It was over. After more than forty minutes hiding for my life in a closet, I slowly began to set my feet on the ground, but I unintentionally stumbled and fell onto a nearby desk with my arms raised. They immediately pointed their guns at me, and for that split second I felt fear reenter my chest. I began to feel paralyzed once again as I looked down the barrel of the gun. I shut my eyes tightly, awaiting their next move, but as quickly as they pointed their guns at me, they lowered them and reunited me with my classmates on the other side of the room. I must have startled them; they must not have noticed me in the closet beforehand.

Relieved and grateful to be alive, I fell into my friends' arms, weak and teary-eyed. They hugged me as we cried together, thankful that I wasn't harmed and that I was safe. When I looked beyond their loving arms, I saw that one of my classmates had blood splattered along his face. "Shards of glass hit him," someone explained from within the group of students. My heart sank and knots began to form in my stomach.

As I looked upon the faces of the students who were in the room with me, I saw Mrs. Lippel. She was with the students she had sheltered in her classroom. I was relieved to see that she was safe, and that others had made it to safety as well. How could this be fake? How could they allow a student to be injured during a drill? This must be real. Please don't let anyone be dead.

The officers began standing us up in order to evacuate the building. When I rose from the classroom floor, I looked out the exit of our classroom and witnessed a grown man, just outside, lying on his back, covered in blood. He had likely been shot after rescuing students from the gunman's fatal bullets, risking his own life. I began crying more intensely as Mrs. Lippel begged me not to look at his dead body. I think she had recognized the man, and she began crying as well.

When instructed to evacuate the room, I remembered my cell phone, which was still recording. The officer demanded that I stay where I was and forget my personal belongings, but without second thought, I apologized for my disobedience and ran to retrieve it anyway.

We were then evacuated from the room in a single-file line with our hands raised. Leaving the classroom, we saw that blood, glass, paper, shattered cell phones, and pieces of wall coated the hallway, and lifeless bodies were strewn along the floor. Smoke still lingered from the shot-up walls. I could hardly hear my own cries of agony over the screams of other students as we all looked upon the dead bodies of friends who had been brutally murdered. I nearly slipped in the blood that stained the hallway as I was being shoved toward the exit at the other end of the hall. The officers instructed us to continue moving and to look down, keeping our hands raised.

I couldn't help but look. It was the most disturbing experience I had ever endured. Though out of respect for those who have lost so much during the shooting, I have decided to exclude specific details of what I witnessed, to keep them private. Not a single person deserved to be lying there on the floor. Nobody deserved to have to walk through that hallway observing everything that had happened while we remained safe and hidden. It was traumatizing for all of us, and I will never be able to remove the bloodstained images from my mind.

On my way out, I saw someone lying by the bathroom door. After passing this particular body, I realized it was my friend Guac. He appeared to have been trying to get into the bathroom during the shooting to seek safety, but the door had been locked by students who ran in before him. The heart that he had taped to his "pinky peach" shirt had fallen off and was lying beside him, no longer pink but dark red.

We were forced to keep moving, and as we walked past the girls' bathroom, I saw two dead girls holding each other facedown. Like Guac, the girls had been trying to enter a different bathroom but were unable to reach safety because of students who had already locked the door before they were able to enter.

It finally dawned on me that this was, in fact, real. I couldn't be in denial anymore. I opened my eyes to the reality that surrounded me, and I grew weak. I felt light-headed as pain raced through my body. It was an intense pain I had never felt before, the pain of losing lives tragically. Experiencing death like this killed something inside me, transforming my fear into rage. What kind of sick human being would do this? How could someone think it necessary to kill innocent people? Children!

As I was running down the stairs to get to the first-floor exit, I saw a pair of ear protectors. They must have been from the gunman, to protect his ears from loud noises made by the guns as he shot my classmates. It made me sick that while he was murdering innocent students, he was protecting his ears from his own destruction.

I made it to the first floor, but before exiting, I turned around and saw numerous bodies in piles along the hall. It pained me to see the terror the gunman had created, but I couldn't keep my eyes from looking. I needed to pay my respects to the room, before it was all nothing more than a tragic memory lost in time.

As I walked outside, I felt the warmth of the sun on my face, and tears fell from my eyes in despair for what we had lost. Piercing sirens and shrieking voices drowned me, putting me in an aimless trance. It felt as though I was walking into a crowd of faces I couldn't recognize, yet they were the same faces I had seen every day since school began. It felt as if my world was on fire, but I was emotionally numb and continued walking as if in a dream. A dream from which I was unable to awaken.

Remembering my cell phone, I reached into my pocket to turn off the recording I had been making. Realizing I only had 8 percent battery left, I immediately attempted to call my father. The first words he said to me were, "Oh my God, Mady, thank God! I love you! Thank God!" Since I was unable to answer my texts during the shooting, my family thought I had been murdered, or at least injured enough to be unable to respond.

I began to cry harder hearing my father's voice. I wasn't crying because I was alive; I was crying because I never had the chance to say goodbye that morning. I never told him I loved him, and I never even gave him a hug before leaving the house. I just left, and had I not made it out, I would never have had the chance to say it again.

Knowing the answers to my following questions, I still felt the need to ask: "Dad, was this real? Are they really dead? Was this not a drill?" And he replied sorrowfully, "It's all over the news. This was real, Mady. I'm so glad you're okay." When he spoke those words, I fell to my knees and dropped my cell phone at my side. I couldn't bear it. Even though part of me had known this was real, another part of me kept hoping it had all been a very elaborate drill. There was no denying the truth now. All I could do was scream.

I picked up my cell phone from the ground and begged my father to come get me, but he was being blocked off by police on the other side of the school and was unable to reach me. So I told him I would find Caitlyn, my twin sister, and come meet him. I knew she was safe because her teacher had been absent from school that day, so her substitute had taken her class to the auditorium, which was far from the Freshman Building.

I impatiently waited for a chance to get to the other side of the road, where a group of students had been evacuated. I didn't know for sure if my sister was in that group, but I couldn't see her on my side of the road.

Before my cell phone battery ran out of power, I scrolled through the dozens of frantic messages from my family—every one of them begging that I answer. "Mady, please tell me you're okay." "Mady, please answer your phone!" "Mady, keep your head down, everything's going to be okay, please talk to me!" It killed me to read them. Some even stated that they thought I was dead, and that if I truly hadn't made it, that they just wanted me to know that they love me. I replied only to my immediate family members, saying that I was safe and that I would call them as soon as I could charge my cell phone.

Finally, I ran to an officer who was eager to help reunite me with my sister. He had me sit on a red mat, gave me a plastic cup of water, and asked me if I had witnessed anything specific. I told him what I had seen, and he got an FBI agent to record the information I had just given for a second time. Eventually the agent had gathered all he could and waited beside me until the students were escorted to the other side of the road. I was unable to find my sister in the mass of students, and I began to panic.

Suddenly I heard someone come up from behind me. It was Caitlyn; she was crying and immediately hugged me. She exclaimed, "I thought you were dead!" I began to cry along with her as she expressed her relief at seeing me again. She held my hand as we waited for the crowd to clear up before walking down a local road nearly a mile away from Stoneman Douglas. I called my dad and told him to meet us away from the school in order to avoid traffic.

One thing Caitlin and I spoke about as we walked, which I will never forget, was her fear that if I had died, she would be without her twin . . . that a piece of her would have died with me. I tried to explain to her what I had witnessed, but it was too excruciating to talk about again so soon.

When we arrived at the location I agreed upon with my father, an older woman was waiting there as well and asked me if I knew her daughter and if she was okay, but I didn't recognize the name and I explained to her that I was unsure of where she might have been. The woman fell into my arms crying and screaming that she only wanted to see her daughter. I told her to walk back toward the school to try to find her.

After speaking with the woman, a younger woman with a camera asked if I would speak to her news crew about what happened. I agreed to tell them what happened so they could share my experience with the public. She warned me not to mention any names while on camera but to just try to relax and answer her questions as clearly as possible. I did my best under the circumstances.

After being interviewed on the local news, my sister and I started to search for our father. Finally we saw his car and immediately climbed in. My dad was so relieved to see us both. He turned around to take us home. As we drove, I told him about what had happened, and he updated me on what he had heard on the news. Shortly after we got home, we learned that the gunman was named Nick Cruz.

It's unfathomable to me that almost two weeks have passed and I am still shaking from the memories. I continue to have nightmares where I'm running through my school being chased by a gunman as he shoots in my direction. He continues to miss until he finds me hiding in the same closet where I hid during the shooting. In the bitter silence within the dream, I shut my eyes in hopes that when I reopen them, I will be safe. When I hear footsteps outside the closet door, I open my eyes and he is looking back at me through the crack in the closet door, and he smiles widely before pulling the trigger. I wake up in tears and covered in sweat. My dad calls them night terrors. I describe them as something nobody should be forced to experience.

In another dream that haunts me, I am being evacuated from the Freshman Building, but when I am released outside, I am completely alone. After running to the opposite side of the road, I turn around. Peering up at the building, I see the seventeen victims staring back at me from the windows. Their eyes are entirely white, without irises, and their bodies completely coated with blood. After I look up at them for a moment, trembling with fear, they raise their arms to point at me. Their faces begin to contort as they vanish from the windows while lowering their arms. My chest suddenly feels tighter, and before I have a chance to run, the gunman is standing behind me with his gun raised to the back of my neck. When I turn to face him, he shows no emotion, and as I begin to scream, he pulls the trigger. Suddenly, all I am able to see is nothingness, leading into black.

I can't imagine the pain the families must be enduring, having lost their loved ones. To send your child off to school to learn, in what you thought was a safe, happy environment, and then to hear that there's been a shooting and your child did not make it to safety—I cannot begin to fathom the amount of suffering they must be living through.

When I saw the picture of the psychopath responsible for all this pain, my heart ached. His emotionless face sickened me. If I ever met him, I'd say, "Are you happy with what you've accomplished? Were you satisfied having murdered my classmates and fellow students? That you shattered seventeen families? How can you live with yourself? You are no human being to me. You are a psychotic murderer. You are no better than scum under the earth, and I hope you rot in hell for what you've done."

Since the shooting, it has been extremely difficult to stay positive, though I've been working to stay motivated in my day-to-day activities. Returning to work has been one of the most helpful tools in distracting myself from what happened, if only for a few hours. I've written each of the seventeen names, whose lives were stolen, on the mirror in my bedroom. Each day I can commemorate and reflect on them and their bravery. Among the seventeen names is Helena. My dear friend was shot during that brutal attack, and through a mutual friend, I heard that she passed away in the hospital. She, like so many others, was taken unfairly and horrifically that dreadful day.

Another friend of mine, Meadow, was shot protecting her friend from open fire. They were both murdered heartlessly by the gunman on the third floor. Meadow and I had two classes together. She had been a role model for me in economics class since the first day of school. While many of the students in that class weren't really focused on their education, Meadow always did everything needed to benefit from the information being presented to her. And she was in creative writing with me when the shooting took place. At the time, she was working on the class assignment—to write a love letter or a love-to-hate letter. She was an astonishing writer, and I loved reading her work. It was tragic that she was never recognized for the inspiring pieces she wrote. My teacher, Mrs. Lippel, would agree that Meadow possessed a remarkable talent for writing. It's excruciating that she will never be able to develop that special ability in what should have been a long and wonderful life. And she will never have the chance to say "I made it."

Unfortunately, Guac and I never had an out-of-school friendship, but during the two classes we shared, we always had a great time. He was always amusing to be around. He had this color in him that somehow made darkness bleed into light, allowing him to find the good in even the most challenging things. Guac and I liked to tease each other over our hair—I thought he was lucky to be blessed with black hair, but he was envious of my blond hair. I'd asked him, "Why would you want to dye your hair blond when you have such beautiful black hair?" And he would laugh and say, "Why would you dye your hair black when you have such beautiful blond hair?"

He also liked to tease me over the ten dollars I owed him after I bet him five dollars that he couldn't flip a water bottle. To my surprise, he did it effortlessly. I talked him into a double-or-nothing arrangement, and he flipped the bottle for the second time, flawlessly. On February 14, I had a twenty-dollar bill to give him, but he told me to wait until the next day so he could bring me change. Then, like so many others, he never saw "the next day."

I wish there was something more I could have done. I felt like a coward for selfishly hiding while others were running for their lives. I wish I hadn't taken another regular day at high school for granted. There is so much I regret about that day, and there are a thousand things I could say about what happened or how I felt, but at some point, words don't help.

It's ironic to me that I had carelessly skipped so many of Mrs. Lippel's classes prior to the shooting, and that I even contemplated skipping it that day. I could have avoided the entire incident had I slacked off and simply returned home. It makes me feel guilty to wish I hadn't been there, though I would give anything to have left when I had the chance.

It was inconceivable to me that anything like this would ever happen to us. You never realize how easily the life you've been given can be torn away from you, even on Valentine's Day, a day when people come together to express their love and compassion for one another. I want to believe that people will walk away from this catastrophe stronger than before. That maybe we won't be so careless with our lives. Maybe we will choose to look at the world around us with a more caring eye. I am optimistic that Nikolas Cruz will suffer immeasurably, and I hope he is repulsed by his actions and loathes himself forevermore. I know I would.

Always Here
By Brianna Jesionowski

The tweeting of the birds,
The heat of the sun,
The whisper of the wind,
The crashing of the waves,
The flowers blowing in the breeze,
The snowflakes falling on your nose,
The raindrops on your window,
The sweet dreams at night,
They are there,
With us every moment of every day,
Our 17 Angels are all of these,
And so much more,
They may not be here physically,
But they are spiritually.

Painting by Lyliah Skinner

Life's Downs
By Brianna Jesionowski

People say life has ups and downs,
They warn you,
But never about this,
My friends died that day,

Blood was shed in vain,
Screaming was heard for miles,
School was supposed to be safe,
But 17 people died that day,
This shouldn't have been a down in life,
I shouldn't worry about living everyday,
A school shooting changed my life,
Afraid I'll never see my friends when I
leave their presence,
Expressing my love for them every time,
In case it is the last,

Life's downs shouldn't include a school
shooting.

Photo by Kyra Parrow

17 Angels

By Brianna Jesionowski

17 Angels of God,
Gone too soon,
Beautiful as can be,
Now singing a sweet tune,
No more pain or worry to feel,
Sweetest people to have known.

17 Angels of God,
In our hearts forever,
Never to be Forgotten,
Missed endlessly.

17 Angels of God,
Shining their light above,
Shining their blessing down upon us,
Free from pain,
Free from fear,
Whose pearly light protects from the darkness
of the night.

Photo by Kevin Trejos

Yoga and Art Heal Our Hearts
by Amy Kenny, yoga instructor at MSD

I was traveling last summer in Denver and came across one of Kelsey Montague's murals, with little heart wings flying off the side of a building. Of course I took some yoga pictures in front of the mural. Then I looked up the hashtag, #whatliftsyou, and immediately connected with Kelsey's work.

At the start of the 2017–18 school year, my yoga program at MSD had grown to well over three hundred students. I was able to start a project to create an outdoor yoga area for my students and was planning to have students create murals or get some local artists to come use our walls as their "canvas" to bring color and art to our site. We had seen a few artists, and the plans were beginning to fall into place to start working after the New Year.

On February 14, I was outside the 1200 building with my students all day by these walls. We had made "random acts of valentines"—cutout foam hearts with encouraging handwritten sayings in marker—to give to the kids at school who seemed lonely or sad. We even gave one to Coach Feis, who had joined us for a few moments on his golf cart. He took a valentine that said "You're cute," smirked, and said, "I know."

An hour later, tragedy struck. Thankfully, my students and I had already gone inside for the day and were in safe places

within the school. But seventeen were left dead and seventeen injured. Our community was broken. I was broken.

After the tragedy, our school was closed for almost two weeks. The day after the attack, the recreation center at Pine Trails Park had set up a counseling area, and a memorial was begun. I spent the day there with students, hugging them, holding vigils, and accompanying them to counseling if they requested. During that time, many of my students reached out and asked me to hold yoga classes to help them and their families to cope with their anxiety and grief. So I held yoga classes in the park every day until school reopened. Hundreds of people came out. Some did yoga, some just sat and cried, but we were together and were beginning the process of healing. Community members, leaders, and people of all ages came together to do yoga because it made them feel better, and for some, it even enabled them to leave their homes for the first time since the tragedy.

During our time together at the park, my students hugged

me and told me stories of how yoga and meditation have helped them get through these difficult days. Some told me they used their breathing techniques during the attacks to remain calm. One student texted me the night of the attack and told me he used his tie-dyed yoga shirt from his backpack as a tourniquet around a girl's leg after she was shot. He saved her life with that yoga shirt, and he told me that it also reminded him to breathe and stay calm as they waited for help to arrive.

Together with a dear friend, Jodi Friedman, we created a nonprofit called Yoga4MSD to raise money for the outdoor space, to send students to yoga teacher training, and to send students on yoga retreats. I continued to hold classes and raise money and awareness of the benefit of yoga for healing trauma.

On April 6, Publix supermarkets came to MSD to beautify our campus and plant trees, lay sod, and build a fountain in my new outdoor yoga studio. Over fifty Publix employees volunteered their time, and Publix donated the materials to create the space.

One of my yoga students was murdered in the attack at MSD. Every day I laid out Meadow Pollack's yoga mat under the trees and placed a journal on it for the students to write in. One day I took a picture for Meadow's aunt Randy and cousin Becca. They said to look at how the leaves of the tree created a big butterfly shadow. They said, "It's Meadow." Those shadow wings reminded me of the murals I had loved in Denver and Kelsey Montague's hashtag, #whatliftsyou.

I said to Jodi, "I wonder if Kelsey Montague would come paint our walls at MSD. . . . I love her work and its meaning, and I think it could help our students begin to heal." Jodi reached out to Kelsey and her sister and business partner, Courtney, to tell our story, and within days they traveled to Parkland to donate their time, materials, and talent to create three beautiful murals.

Little did we know that Kelsey and Courtney were from Littleton, Colorado, where the shooting at Columbine took place. The sisters' schools were both in lockdown during the attack that day. Having lived through a similar tragedy, our story really connected with them. They felt compelled to come help our community heal through art.

We are forever grateful to Kelsey and Courtney for our special walls. The walls pay tribute to Meadow and her love for yoga. These murals have also brought back smiles and laughter to our campus while we continue to heal and reclaim our school.

Photo by Amy Kenny

#WhatLiftsYou

Photo by Elisa Williamson

Just Breathe

BY AMY KENNY, YOGA INSTRUCTOR AT MSD

Yoga
mind, body, and soul
My mat is a safe haven from the storms of life
The breath is my anchor
Guiding my body through the dance of meditation
No thoughts . . . just breath . . . with movement
Moving energy out of my body
Healing these fresh wounds of my heart
Banishing the darkness
Feeding my soul
Illuminating awareness
Light

Photo by Amy Kenny

RESOURCES

If you or someone you know needs help with grief, anxiety, depression, or PTSD, there are numerous websites, organizations, and support networks. Below are just a few of those resources.

HOTLINES

National Alliance on Mental Illness
800-950-NAMI (6264)
Trained volunteers provide information, referrals, and support to anyone with questions about mental illness.

National Suicide Prevention Lifeline
800-273-TALK (8255)
A 24-hour service available to anyone in need of help.

National Youth Crisis Hotline
800-448-4663
Provides short-term counseling for youth in various crises.

Substance Abuse and Mental Health Services Administration (SAMHSA)
800-662-HELP (4357)
Provides 24-hour services for individuals and family members facing mental health and substance use disorders.

WEBSITES

The Dougy Center: The National Center for
Grieving Children & Families
Provides support in a safe place where teens and their families
can grieve and share their experiences.
dougy.org/grief-resources/help-for-teens

Hospice of the Valley, Teen Grief Support
Provides help and counseling to teens who are working through
grief.
hov.org/teen-grief-support

National Alliance on Mental Illness (NAMI)
A grassroots organization for people with mental illness and their
families.
nami.org

Sandy Hook Promise
Providing information on school safety, including guidance on
how to recognize the signs of at-risk behavior.
sandyhookpromise.org

SAVE (Students Against Violence Everywhere)
Providing teens with the opportunity to show leadership,
creativity, and passion by protecting their friends, schools, and
communities from violence before it happens.
nationalsave.org

Society for the Prevention of Teen Suicide
Encourages public awareness through the development and
promotion of educational training programs.
sptsusa.org

BOOKS

Beyond the Blues: A Workbook to Help Teens Overcome Depression, by Lisa M. Schab, Oakland, CA: Instant Help, 2008.

Hello, Cruel World: 101 Alternatives to Suicide for Teens, Freaks, and Other Outlaws, by Kate Bornstein, New York: Seven Stories Press, 2006.

How I Resist: Activism and Hope for a New Generation, by Maureen Johnson, New York: Wednesday Books, 2018.

If You Feel Too Much, by Jamie Tworkowski, New York: TarcherPerigee, 2016.

My Anxious Mind: A Teen's Guide to Managing Anxiety and Panic, by Michael A. Tompkins and Katherine Martinez, Washington, DC: Magination, 2009.

#NeverAgain: A New Generation Draws the Line, by David Hogg and Lauren Hogg, New York: Random House, 2018.

Staying Strong: 365 Days a Year, by Demi Lovato, New York: Feiwel and Friends, 2013.

MEET THE CONTRIBUTORS

*Note: All ages reflect the contributor's school year on February 14, 2018.

Suzanna Barna (senior) was a first-year staffer for the *Eagle Eye* and a member of the National Honor Society, the Key Club, and various other clubs at school. She was also known for hosting a community service program for the senior citizens at Aston Gardens. Suzanna will study civil engineering and business administration at the University of Florida in the fall, and plans to write for the student-run publication the *Alligator*.

Anna Bayuk (junior) is co-president of MSD's Spoken Word Club, has been featured on NBC6, and has competed statewide in the Louder Than a Bomb poetry competition. She lives in Coral Springs, Florida.

Samantha Bonnin (senior) served as both an editor for MSD's *Artifex* literary magazine and president for the Spoken Word Club. She has loved words ever since she heard her first story and sees writing as an outlet to both express her feelings and allow her creativity to run free. After the events of February 14, 2018, she turned to writing to work through the stages of her grief. Samantha will attend Northeastern University in Boston, where she will pursue a degree in English and continue to grow as a writer.

Grace Briden (sophomore) moved to Florida this past year, after living in four other countries over nine years. She is the oldest of five kids and is originally from Portage, Michigan. She's very excited to have more adventures in life!

Chantal Chalita (senior) will attend the University of Miami and hopes to major in graphic design and minor in journalism and marketing. During her four years at MSD, Chantal served as a writer, content editor, and co-editor-in-chief on the yearbook staff. In her free time, Chantal enjoys playing the piano and guitar, singing, reading, and writing.

Joseph DeArce (sophomore) aspires to become a fiction writer one day. In the meantime, he spends his days playing video games with friends or being with his family in Parkland, where he's lived all his life.

Samantha Deitsch (freshman) is a junior varsity cheerleader, vice president of social affairs at the largest youth group in the Parkland area, and a part of March For Our Lives, an organization that is determined to end gun violence. Samantha is an activist working to create a better world.

Taylor Ferrante-Markham (junior) was a twice-published author—in *Scholastic* magazine and MSD's literary magazine—before she turned eighteen. Addicted to iced hazelnut coffee and guacamole, Taylor hopes to study journalism and education at St. John's University in New York after she graduates from MSD in 2019 in order to be closer to her crazy big Italian family.

Brianna Fisher (sophomore) is a first-year staff writer for the *Eagle Eye*. She was the freshman class president and a sophomore class senator and is an incoming junior class senator. Brianna is also a member of the Math Honor Society, the National English Honor Society, and the National Association of Students Against Gun Violence. She was a morale captain for Dance Marathon in 2017–18 and is the partnership chair on the executive board for 2018–19. Brianna plans to double major in political science and criminology and minor in cognitive psychology in college.

Alexis Gendron (junior) enjoys yoga and hopes to pursue a career in holistic medicine. After she graduates in 2019, she plans to move to Utah for a fresh start and to attend college.

Emma González (senior) helped start and organize the March For Our Lives on March 24 after Marjory Stoneman Douglas High School experienced a shooting on Valentine's Day. The people who were lost on that day, the ones who were injured, and the ones who will never forget the atrocity committed are why she fights for gun reform. She enjoys sewing, crocheting, reading, singing, and drawing. She's interested in outer space, environmental science, and art. She will attend New College of Florida, and plans to major in whatever will help make the world a better place.

Augustus Griffith Jr. (junior) is a devout writer from Parkland. He is the secretary of the school's TV Production club, and he recently published his first ebook, *Running in Circles: A Poetry Collection*.

Sam Grizelj (sophomore) has been involved in the TV Production program for two years and took on the role of producer in their second class. Sam has taken on their own projects, such as creating a promotional video for the Parkland Buddy Sports program, and many more. When Sam is not working on a major project, they're working on their photography skills and continuing to improve their filming skills.

Brianna Jesionowski (freshman) comes from a military household that moves a lot. She started at MSD in 2017. She is interested in writing, photography, and modeling, and plans to major in social work in college.

Anna Kasperski (freshman) took first place in the Broward County Public Schools 2017 Literary Fair for her sonnet "Getting Lost in a Book." Despite the seven-year age difference, she has an incredibly tight bond with her twenty-two-year-old sister Kate— who also experienced gun violence, at Florida State University in 2014. While traveling, Anna enjoys capturing her experience through writing and photography.

Amy Kenny is a passionate yogi who has transformed her life through yoga. As an athlete and triathlete, she uses yoga to stay flexible when training and stay balanced emotionally and spiritually. As a high school English teacher, she saw the need for mindfulness and yoga in the schools and became a certified yoga instructor and a certified physical education teacher. She left her job teaching English to teach a full schedule of yoga to over 300 students and athletes at Marjory Stoneman Douglas High School.

Hayden Korr (senior) enjoys writing, photography, and 2-D art. Her work has been published in MSD's literary magazine *Artifex,* and featured on the album covers of the L.A. band It's Butter.

Sarah Lerner is an English teacher, journalism teacher, and yearbook adviser at Marjory Stoneman Douglas High School (MSD). She began teaching in 2002 and came to MSD in 2014. Prior to MSD, she was named the *Sun-Sentinel* High School Journalism Teacher of the Year. Sarah lives with her husband and two children. In her free time, she likes to read, crochet, blog, travel, and spend time with her family.

Sara Lesmes (freshman) plans to study science and hopes to pursue a career in that field. She also enjoys writing and painting in her free time.

Stacey Lippel has been a Broward County teacher for thirteen years, the last five at MSD, where she teaches English and creative writing. She also advises the school's Spoken Word Club. Sarah enjoys cooking, working out, and participating in an active lifestyle with her husband and seventeen-year-old twins, who attend MSD.

Jack Macleod (junior) has taken creative writing for the past three years and will be joining the *Eagle Eye* newspaper staff next year. Jack is one of the founders of Students 4 Change and is a founder and executive board member of the Student Gun Violence Summit. He is an avid video game player, has a tight group of friends, and loves listening to music.

Alyssa Marrero (sophomore) started at MSD in her sophomore year. She is an only child who loves her dad and misses her mom, who passed away when Alyssa was fifteen. She has two adorable Yorkies whom she loves and cherishes. In the future, Alyssa plans to attend New York University or the University of Southern California and aspires to be a director in the film industry. She hopes to someday travel around the world, and her greatest wish is to make her mother proud.

Natasha Martinez (junior) is a member of the *Aerie* yearbook staff, where she is both the clubs and captions editor. She is also a member of Mu Alpha Theta, the Spanish Club, the French Club, and Best Buddies. She enjoys painting and spending time with family and friends. She plans to study either biomedical engineering or journalism in college.

Nadia Murillo (freshman) plays varsity water polo for MSD and for the City of Coral Springs Water Polo Club. During her sophomore year, she will be a staff writer for the school newspaper, the *Eagle Eye*. Nadia is also a member of the school's DECA chapter and the Key Club. She is passionate about journalism and has taken an interest in the political change of our country. When she's not busy with water polo, Nadia can be found with her friends or sipping on a matcha latte.

Daniela Ortiz-Machado (junior) was a content editor of her school yearbook in 2018 and will be a content editor and co-editor-in-chief in her senior year. She hopes to become a journalist one day. Aside from writing, she loves fashion, reading, watching movies, and listening to music.

Kyra Parrow (senior) is a self-taught photographer with more than five years of experience behind the camera. She served as the photo editor of the *Aerie,* the MSD yearbook, for three years and as its editor-in-chief for two years. Her work has been published in *Elle* and *Time* magazines. Her photography after the shooting helped her process her grief through art.

Aly Peri (junior) will play her fourth year of varsity football this year. She plans to attend Florida State University next year and aspires to work with children in the future. After the events of February 14, Aly realized writing is the best way to cope with her grief and take out her anger.

Isabella Pfeiffer (junior) has been living in Parkland since she was eight years old. She witnessed how mass shootings can absolutely destroy towns and people's hearts, and she is focused on making sure it never happens again. She is a member of Students 4 Change and is a founding member of the Student Gun Violence Summit.

Kaitlyn Puller (sophomore) has been interested in writing since she was in elementary school, and her love for creative writing has only grown over the years. She also plays the piano and is a keyboardist in a band.

Danielle Rittman (sophomore) has lived in Parkland all of her life. She enjoys dance class at Dance Theatre of Parkland and was a member of the Dance Theatre Company, a performance team. Danielle is passionate about helping others, which is one of the reasons she chaired the Dance Marathon at MSD, a national student organization that raises money for kids fighting illness. She is also the business manager of MSD's yearbook. Danielle loves to have fun with her friends and travel with her family.

Alejandro Rodriguez (sophomore) aspires to become a heart surgeon. He also has a passion for cars. Alejandro has a less serious side and enjoys playing video games, going to the movies, and spending time with friends at the beach and the park.

Chloe Rogers (freshman) enjoys taking pictures of the outside world, playing soccer, and writing poems and short stories. She plays travel soccer for Coral Springs United and flag football for the MSD team. Chloe also loves to bake and read and spend time laughing at videos with her friends.

Kaleela Rosenthal (freshman) has lived in Coral Springs and Parkland her whole life but considers Puerto Rico her home away from home. She enjoys listening to music, traveling, and experiencing new things. She is planning to pursue a career in helping others, big or small.

Rebecca Schneid (junior) is a second-year staff member of the *Eagle Eye* and served as co-editor-in-chief in the 2017–18 school year. She is also an officer of the Politics Club, the Key Club, and the Spanish Honor Society, and has been a member of the National Honor Society, the National English Honor Society, and the Math Honor Society. While Rebecca has a passion for biology, she has found her true calling in political science and journalism, where she enjoys writing hard-hitting features.

Ryan Servaites (freshman) is an activist and going into his fourth year of debate team. He enjoys philosophy, political theory, literature, and music. Ryan has played guitar for three years, and his favorite book is *Animal Farm.*

Alyson Sheehy (senior) is a member of the National Honor Society, the Key Club, the varsity softball team, and the yearbook staff. Alyson plans to attend the University of Central Florida and aspires to work in the field of pediatric medicine. After the events of February 14, Alyson found writing and drawing to be the best way to heal her pain and take out her frustration.

Lyliah Skinner (junior) is going into her third year on the *Aerie* yearbook staff and her second year as the sports editor. She enjoys traveling, art and photography, tweeting, and trying new foods.

Madalyn Snyder (junior) graduated early from MSD. After working as a barn manager on multiple horse training and breeding farms for the past three and a half years, she hopes to further her education in equestrian studies. Since February 14, 2018, Madalyn has concentrated on her passion for drawing in hopes of having a side business in the tattoo industry. She is grateful for her life and has made it a priority to never let an opportunity slip by.

Leni Steinhardt (sophomore) is a first-year staff writer for the *Eagle Eye*. She is a member of Students Demand Action, the National Association of Students Against Gun Violence, and the girls' varsity golf team, and is treasurer of the National English Honor Society. She is also the marketing and publicity chair and morale captain of Dance Marathon, the historian of her local BBYO chapter, and a freshman class senator. Leni is a two-year recipient of the Underclassman Award for Journalism and Newspaper and hopes to major in journalism and mass communication in college and pursue a career in the field.

Caitlynn Tibbetts (sophomore) lives in Coral Springs, where she can often be found at the gym with her father, cuddled in her bedroom reading a scary murder mystery, or listening to Harry Styles and BTS. Caitlynn has two cats, Bubbles and Pumpkin, and a dog